IMPROVE YOUR READING

SIXTH EDITION

Ron Fry

Course Technology PTR

A part of Cengage Learning

COURSE TECHNOLOGY
CENGAGE Learning·

Australia, Brazil, Japan, Korea, Mexico, Singapore, Spain, United Kingdom, United States

COURSE TECHNOLOGY
CENGAGE Learning·

**Improve Your Reading,
Sixth Edition
Ron Fry**

**Publisher and General Manager,
Course Technology PTR:**
Stacy L. Hiquet

**Associate Director of
Marketing:**
Sarah Panella

Manager of Editorial Services:
Heather Talbot

Marketing Manager:
Mark Hughes

Senior Acquisitions Editor:
Mitzi Koontz

Interior Layout Tech:
Judy Littlefield

Cover Designer:
Luke Fletcher

Indexer:
Larry D. Sweazy

Proofreader:
Sandi Wilson

Library of Congress Control Number: 2011940743

ISBN-13: 978-1-4354-6106-2

ISBN-10: 1-4354-6106-1

Course Technology, a part of Cengage Learning
20 Channel Center Street
Boston, MA 02210
USA

Cengage Learning is a leading provider of customized learning solutions with office locations around the globe, including Singapore, the United Kingdom, Australia, Mexico, Brazil, and Japan. Locate your local office at: **international.cengage.com/region**.

Cengage Learning products are represented in Canada by Nelson Education, Ltd.

For your lifelong learning solutions, visit **courseptr.com**.

Visit our corporate website at **cengage.com**.

Printed by RR Donnelley.
Crawfordsville, IN. 1st Ptg. 11/2011

Printed in the United States of America
1 2 3 4 5 6 7 13 12 11

CONTENTS

FOREWORD

READ ON!

A number of you are students, not just the high school students I always thought were my readers, but also college students making up for study skills you may have lacked in high school, and middle school students trying to master these study skills early in your educational career to maximize your opportunities for success.

If you're a high school student, you should be particularly comfortable with both the language and format of this book—its relatively short sentences and paragraphs, occasionally humorous (hopefully) headings and subheadings, and a reasonable but certainly not outrageous vocabulary. I wrote it with you in mind!

If you're a middle school student, I doubt you'll have trouble with the concepts or language in this book. Sixth, seventh, and eighth grade is the perfect time to learn the different ways to read and the methods to better retain whatever you're reading. You're probably just discovering that *The Babysitter's Club* series is not what your parents or teachers had in mind when they encouraged you to read "the classics."

And if you are a "traditional" college student, age 18 to 25, I would have hoped that you had already mastered most, if not all, of the basic study skills, especially reading and writing. Since you haven't, please make learning, using, and mastering all of the study skills covered in my *How to Study Program* an absolute priority.

Do not pass "Go." Do not go on a date. Take the time to learn these skills now. You may have been able to kid yourself that mediocre or even poor reading skills didn't stop you from finishing, perhaps even succeeding in, high school. I guarantee you will not be able to kid anyone in college. You must master all of the skills in this book to survive, let alone succeed.

If You Finished School Long Ago

Many of you reading this are adults. Some of you are returning to school, and some of you are long out of school but have figured out that if you can learn now the study skills your teachers never taught you, you'll do better in your careers—especially if you are able to read what you need to faster...and retain it better and longer.

All too many of you are parents with the same lament: "How do I get Johnny to do better in school? He thinks the Sunday comics are the height of literature."

Your child's school is probably doing little, if anything, to teach him or her how to study, which means he or she is not learning how to learn. And that means he or she is not learning how to succeed.

Should the schools be accomplishing that? Absolutely. We ought to be getting more for our money than a diploma, some football cheers, and a rotten entry-level job market.

What Can Parents Do?

Okay, here they are, the rules for parents of students of any age:

1. **Set up a homework area.** Free of distraction, well lit, with all necessary supplies handy.

2. **Set up a homework routine.** When and where it gets done. Studies have clearly shown that students who establish a regular routine are better organized and, as a result, more successful.

3. **Set homework priorities.** Actually, just make the point that homework is the priority—before a date, before TV, before going out to play, whatever.

4. **Make reading a habit**—for them, certainly, but also for yourselves. Kids will inevitably do what you do, not what you say (even if you say not to do what you do).

5. **Turn off the TV.** Or at the very least, severely limit when and how much TV-watching is appropriate. This may be the toughest suggestion to enforce. I know. I was once the parent of a teenager.

6. **Talk to the teachers.** Find out what your kids are supposed to be learning. If you don't know the books they're supposed to be reading, what's expected of them in class, and how much homework they should be scheduling, you can't really give them the help they need.

7. **Encourage and motivate,** but don't nag them to do their homework. It doesn't work. The more you insist, the quicker they will tune you out.

8. **Supervise their work**, but don't fall into the trap of doing their homework. Checking (i.e., proofreading) a paper, for example, is a positive way to help your child in school. But if you simply put in corrections without your child learning from her mistakes, you're not helping her at all...except in the belief that she is not responsible for her own work.

9. **Praise them when they succeed,** but don't over-praise them for mediocre work. Kids know when you're being insincere and, again, will quickly tune you out.

10. **Convince them of reality.** (This is for older students.) Okay, I'll admit it's almost as much of a stretch as turning off the TV, but learning and believing that the real world will not care about their grades, but will measure them by what they know and what they can do, is a lesson that will save many tears (probably yours). It's probably never too early to (carefully) let your boy or girl genius get the message that life is not fair.

11. **If you can afford it,** get your kid(s) a computer and all the software they can handle. There really is no avoiding it: Your kids, whatever their ages, absolutely must be computer-savvy in order to survive in and after school.

12. **Turn off the TV already!**

13. **Get wired.** The Internet is the greatest invention of our age and an unbelievable tool for students of any age. It is impossible for a college student to succeed without the ability to surf online in this age of technology. They've got to be connected.

14. But turn off IM (Instant Messaging) while doing homework. They will attempt to convince you that they can write a term paper, do their geometry homework, and IM their friends at the same time. Parents who believe this have also been persuaded that the best study area is in front of the TV.

The Importance of Your Involvement

Don't for a minute underestimate the importance of your commitment to your child's success: Your involvement in your child's education is absolutely essential to his or her eventual success. The results of every study done in the last two decades about what affects a child's success in school demonstrate that only one factor overwhelmingly affects it, every time: parental involvement—not the size of the school, the money spent per pupil, the number of language labs, how many of the students go on to college, how many great teachers there are (or lousy ones). All factors, yes. But none as significant as the effect you can have.

You can help tremendously, even if you were not a great student yourself, even if you never learned great study skills. You can learn now with your child—it will help her in school, and it will help you on the job, whatever your field.

If You're a Nontraditional Student

If you're going back to high school, college, or graduate school at age 25, 45, 65, or 85—you probably need the help these books offer more than anyone! As much as I emphasize that it's rarely too early to learn good study habits, I must also emphasize that it's never too late.

If you're returning to school and attempting to carry even a partial load of courses while simultaneously holding down a job, raising a family, or both, there are some particular problems you face that you probably didn't the first time you were in school:

Time and money pressures. Let's face it: When all you had to worry about was going to school, it was easier than going to school, raising a family, and working for a living simultaneously.

Self-imposed fears of inadequacy. You may well convince yourself that you're just "out of practice" with all this school stuff. You don't even remember what to do with a highlighter! While some of this fear is valid, most is not.

The valid part is that you are returning to an academic atmosphere, one that you may not have visited for a decade or two. And it is different (which I'll discuss more next) than the "work-a-day" world. That's just a matter of adjustment and—trust me—it will take a matter of days, if not hours, to dissipate.

I suspect what many of you are really fearing is that you just aren't in that school "mentality" anymore, that you don't "think" the same way. Or, perhaps more pertinent to this book, that the skills you need to succeed in school are rusty.

I think these last fears are groundless. You've been out there thinking and doing for quite a few years, perhaps very successfully, so it's really ridiculous to think school will be so different. It won't be. Relax. And while you may think your study skills are rusty, as we discussed earlier, you've probably been using them every day in your career. Even if I can't convince you, you have my *How to Study Program* as your refresher course. It will probably teach you more about studying than you ever forgot you knew.

Maybe you're worried because you didn't exactly light up the academic world the first time around. Well, neither did Edison or Einstein or a host of other successful people. But then, you've changed rather significantly since then, haven't you? Concentrate on how much more qualified you are for school now than you were then!

Feeling you're "out of your element." This is a slightly different fear, the fear that you just don't fit in any more. After all, you're not 18 again. But then, neither are fully half the college students on campuses today. That's right: Fully 50 percent of all college students are older than 25. The reality is, you'll probably feel more in your element now than you did the first time around!

You'll see teachers differently. Probably a plus. It's doubtful you'll have the same awe you did the first time around. At worst, you'll consider teachers your equals. At best, you'll consider them younger and not necessarily as successful or experienced as you are. In either event, you probably won't be quite as ready to treat your college professors as if they were minor deities.

There are differences in academic life. It's slower than the "real" world, and you may well be moving significantly faster than its normal pace. When you were 18, an afternoon without classes meant a game of Frisbee. Now it might mean catching up on a week's worth of errands, cooking (and freezing) a week's worth of dinners, and/or writing four reports due this week. Despite your own hectic schedule, do not expect campus life to accelerate in response. You will have to get used to people and systems with far less interest in speed.

Some Random Thoughts About Learning

Learning shouldn't be painful and certainly doesn't have to be boring, though it's far too often both. It's not necessarily going to be wonderful and painless, either. Sometimes you actually have to work hard to figure something out or get a project done. That is reality.

It's also reality that everything isn't readily apparent or easily understandable. That's okay. You will learn how to get past the confusion. Heck, if you actually think you're supposed to understand everything you read the first time through, you're kidding yourself. Learning something slowly doesn't mean there's something wrong with you. It may be a subject that virtually everybody learns slowly. A good student just takes his time, follows a reasonable plan, and remains confident that the lightbulb of understanding will eventually click on.

Parents often ask me, "How can I motivate my teenager?" My initial response is usually to smile and say, "If I knew the answer to that question, I would have retired very wealthy quite some time ago." I think there is an answer, but it's not something parents can do—it's something the student has to decide: Are you going to spend the school day interested and alert or bored and resentful?

It's really that simple. Since you have to go to school anyway, why not develop the attitude that you might as well be active and learn as much as possible instead of being miserable? The difference between a C and an A or B for many students is, I firmly believe, merely a matter of wanting to do better. As I constantly stress in radio and TV interviews, inevitably you will leave school. And very quickly, you'll discover all anyone really cares about is what you know and what you can do. Grades won't count anymore; neither will tests. So you can learn it all now or regret it later.

How many times have you said to yourself, "I don't know why I'm bothering trying to learn this calculus (algebra, geometry, physics, chemistry, history, whatever). I'll never use this again!"? The truth is, you have no clue what you're going to need to know tomorrow or next week, let alone next year or in a decade.

I've been amazed in my own life how things I did with no specific purpose in mind (except probably to earn money or meet a girl) turned out years later to be not just invaluable to my life or career, but essential. How was I to know when I took German as my language elective in high school that the most important international trade show in book publishing was in Frankfurt, Germany? Or that the basic skills I learned one year working for an accountant (while I was writing my first book) would become essential when I later started four companies? Or how important basic math skills would be in selling and negotiating over the years? (Okay, I'll admit it: I haven't used a differential equation in 20 years, but, hey, you never know!)

So learn it all. And don't be surprised if the subject you'd vote "least likely to ever be useful" winds up being the key to your fame and fortune.

There Aren't Many Study Rules

Though I immodestly maintain that my *How to Study Program* is the most helpful to the most people, there are certainly plenty of other purported study books out there.

Inevitably, these other books promote the authors' "system," which usually means what they did to get through school. This "system," whether basic and traditional or wildly quirky, may or may not work for you. So what do you do if "their" way of taking notes makes no sense to you? Or you master their highfalutin' "Super Student Study Symbols" and still get Cs?

There are very few "rights" and "wrongs" out there in the study world. There's certainly no single "right" way to attack a multiple choice test or take notes. So don't get fooled into thinking there is, especially if what you're doing seems to be working for you.

Needless to say, don't read my books looking for that single, inestimable system of "rules" that will work for everyone. You won't find it, 'cause there's no such bird. You will find a plethora of techniques, tips, tricks, gimmicks, and what-have-you, some or all of which may work for you, some of which won't. Pick and choose, change and adapt, figure out what works for you. Because you are the one responsible for creating your study system, not me.

I've used the phrase "Study smarter, not harder" as a sort of catch phrase in promotion and publicity for the *How to Study Program* for two decades. So what does it mean to you? Does it mean I guarantee you'll spend less time studying? Or that the least amount of time is best? Or that studying isn't ever supposed to be difficult?

Hardly. It does mean that studying inefficiently is wasting time that could be spent doing other (okay, probably more fun) things and that getting your studying done as quickly and efficiently as possible is a realistic, worthy, and attainable goal. I'm no stranger to hard work, but I'm not a monastic dropout who thrives on self-flagellation. I try not to work harder than I have to!

It's a Hard-Wired World

In 1988, when I wrote the first edition of *How to Study*, I composed it, formatted it, and printed it on (gasp) a personal computer. Most people did not have a computer, let alone a neighborhood network and DSL, or surf the Internet, or chat online, or Instant Message their friends, or read hundreds of books on a Kindle, or...you get the point.

Those days are very dead and gone. And you should cheer, even if you aren't sure what DOS was (is? could be?). Because the spread of the personal computer and, even more important, the Internet, has taken studying from the Dark Ages to the Info Age in merely a decade.

As a result, you will find all of my books assume you have a computer and know how to use it—for note taking, reading, writing papers, researching, and much more. There are many tasks that may be harder on a computer—and I'll point them out—but don't believe for a second that a computer won't help you tremendously, whatever your age, whatever your grades.

As for the Internet, it has absolutely revolutionized research. Whether you're writing a paper, putting together a reading list, studying for the SAT, or just trying to organize your life, it has become a more valuable tool than the greatest library in the world. Heck, it *is* the greatest library in the world...and more. So if you are not Internet-savvy (yes, I'm talking to the parents out there, couldn't you tell?), admit it, get a book (over the Internet, of course), and get wired. You'll be missing far too much—and be studying far harder—without it.

The Last Commerical

Before we get on with all the tips and techniques necessary to make textbooks quake when they see you coming, let me make two important points about all of my study books.

First, I believe in gender equality, but I find constructions such as "he and she," "s/he," "womyn," and other such stretches to be sometimes painfully awkward. I have therefore attempted to sprinkle pronouns of both genders throughout the text.

Second, you will find that many similar pieces of advice, examples, lists, terms, phrases, and sections appear in several of my books. Certainly *How to Study*, which is an overview of all the study skills, necessarily contains, though in summarized form, some of each of the other five books.

The repetition is unavoidable. While I urge everyone to read all the books in the series, but especially *How to Study*, they are six individual books. And many people buy only one of them. Consequently, I must include in each book the pertinent material for that topic, even if that material is repeated in another book.

That said, I can guarantee that the nearly 1,000 pages of my *How to Study Program* contain the most wide-ranging, comprehensive, and complete system of studying ever published. I have attempted to create a system that is usable, useful, practical, and learnable. One that you can use—whatever your age, whatever your level of achievement, whatever your IQ—to start doing better in school, in work, and in life immediately.

Good luck.

Ron Fry

CHAPTER 1

THE BASIS OF ALL STUDY SKILLS

I think you'll find this is a book unlike any you've read before. And if you take the time to read it, I promise it will make everything else you have to read—whatever your student status, whatever your job, whatever your age—a lot easier to get through.

Why? Because I'm going to show you how to plow through all your reading assignments—whatever the subjects—better and faster… and how to remember more of what you read.

This book is not a gimmicky speed-reading method. It's not a spelling and grammar guide. Nor is it a lecture on the joys of reading. It's a practical guide, geared to you—a student of any age who isn't necessarily a poor reader, but who wants to get more from reading and do better in school and in life.

Personally, I'll read just about anything handy, just to be able to read something. But just because I have always loved to read, it didn't make it any easier to face some of those deadly textbook reading assignments. As a student, you will inevitably be required, as I was, to spend hours poring through ponderous, fact-filled, convoluted reading assignments for subjects that are required, but not exactly scintillating.

You may love reading for pleasure but have trouble reading textbook assignments for certain subjects. You may get the reading done but forget what you've read nearly as quickly as you read it. Or you just may hate the thought of sitting still to read anything. Whatever kind of student you are—and whatever your level of reading skill—I've written this book to help you surmount your reading challenge, whatever it may be.

And that includes, for those of you long out of school, reading those nap-inducing business tomes, trade magazine articles, and other work-related stuff that's rarely reader-friendly.

You'll learn what you should read—and what you don't have to. You'll discover how to cut down on the time you spend reading, how to identify the main idea in your reading, as well as the important details, and how to remember more of what you read.

I'll show you different ways to read various types of books, from dry science texts to cumbersome classics.

Who knows? I might even convince you that reading is fun!

When you're a good reader, the world is your oyster—you qualify for better schools, better jobs, better pay. Poor readers qualify for poor jobs and less fulfilling lives.

Ready to Begin? Get Motivated!

Any attempt to improve your reading must begin with motivation. Reading is not a genetic trait that is written in your DNA—there's no gene that makes you a good or bad reader like the ones that decide your hair or eye color. For the most part, reading is an acquired skill—a skill you can secure, grow, and sharpen. You just have to want to.

As the Nike commercial lambastes all of us weekend warriors—"Just Do It!" This attitude—not technique—is where the quest for improved reading begins. You must make reading a habit.

Good Reader vs. Poor Reader

Look at the following comparison of a good reader and a poor reader as if you were some corporate hotshot who could hire just one of the individuals.

Good Reader: You read for purpose. You've clearly defined your reason for reading—a question you want answered, facts you must remember, ideas you need to grasp, current events that affect you, or just the pleasure of following a well-written story.

Poor Reader: Yes, you read, but often have no real reason for doing so. You aimlessly struggle through assigned reading, with little effort to grasp the "message."

Good Reader: You read and digest the concepts and ideas the author is trying to communicate.

Poor Reader: You get lost in the muddle of words, struggling to make sense of what the author is trying to say. You are often bored because you force yourself to read every word to "get the message"…which you usually don't.

Good Reader: You read critically and ask questions to evaluate whether the author's arguments are reasonable or totally off-the-wall. You recognize biases and don't just "believe" everything you read.

Poor Reader: You suffer from the delusion that everything in print is true and are easily swayed from what you formerly believed to be true by any argument that sounds good.

Good Reader: You read a variety of books, magazines, and newspapers and enjoy all types of reading—fiction, poetry, biography, current events.

Poor Reader: You're a one-track reader—you read the sports pages, comics, or Gothic novels. Current events? You catch updates about your world from TV news "sound bites."

Good Reader: You enjoy reading and embrace it as an essential tool in your desire to better yourself.

Poor Reader: You hate to read, deeming it a chore to be endured only when you have to. Reading is "boring."

Take a minute and ask yourself, whom would you hire? Yes, you might hire Mr. Poor Reader…in some low-paying job. But would you ever put someone with such low-level skills in a position of major responsibility?

At this point, I won't ask you to evaluate your own level of reading skills. Characterizing yourself as a "good" or "poor" reader was not the point of this exercise. What is important is to realize that Ms. Good Reader didn't spring full-blown from Zeus's cranium quoting Shakespearean sonnets and reading physics texts for fun. She learned to read the same way you and I did—with "See Spot run."

In time and through making reading a habit, Ms. Good Reader acquired and honed a skill that will open a world of opportunity to her.

Mr. Poor Reader, at some point, decided that being a good reader was not worth the effort and made poor reading his habit.

The good news is that being a poor reader is not a life sentence—you can improve your reading. The challenge is to find the motivation!

How Fast Can You Understand?

When we read too fast or too slowly,
we understand nothing.
—Pascal

Are you worried that you read too slowly? You probably shouldn't be—less rapid readers are not necessarily less able. What counts is what you comprehend and remember. And like anything else, practice will probably increase your speed levels. If you must have a ranking, read the 500-word selection that follows (adapted from *American Firsts* by Stephen Spignesi, published by New Page Books, 2004) from start to finish, noting the elapsed time on your watch. Score yourself as follows:

45 seconds or less	very fast
46–60 seconds	fast
61–90 seconds	high average
91–119 seconds	average
120–150 seconds	slow
151 seconds or more	very slow

The original incarnation of Coca-Cola contained cocaine, a common ingredient of patent medicines in the late 19th century. The drug was so beloved and believed to be so beneficial that the early ads for Coca-Cola pitched it as a "brain tonic." Cocaine did what cocaine does: It made people more alert and focused; it elevated mood (to the point of euphoria); it eliminated fatigue and had something of an analgesic effect. Who knew it was addictive?

Eventually everyone did, and over the past century, the Coca-Cola company has worked very hard to eliminate any traces of cocaine from the beverage. However, cocaine is found in the cola nut (a seed of the coca leaf) and it is therefore impossible to remove it entirely. The amount of cocaine in Coca-Cola is so miniscule, however, as to be immeasurable; by any and all standards, Coca-Cola is cocaine free. It is not caffeine free, though, because this stimulant is also found in the coca leaf and no attempt is made to remove it for regular Coke. It is removed, though, for production of caffeine-free cola beverages.

Coca-Cola is the world's most recognized trademark. Some estimates claim that 94 percent of the world's population recognizes the Coca-Cola name and/or distinctive Spencerian Script logo. The original formula for Coca-Cola syrup was concocted by Dr. John Pemberton in his Atlanta, Georgia backyard in early May 1885. (Today, the secret formula of Coke is known as "7X.") He used a three-legged kettle, and his bookkeeper Frank Robinson not only came up with the name, but also drew the first script version of the product's name. The syrup was mixed with water and first sold to the thirsty at the soda fountain in Jacob's Pharmacy in Atlanta on May 8, 1885. It was touted as a brain and nerve tonic, but Pemberton lost money in his first year selling the drink.

Legend has it that Pemberton saw one of his employees adding carbonated seltzer water to the "tonic," and the Coke we know today was born. Today, Coca-Cola is the most popular beverage in the world. More than one billion Cokes are consumed every day, and it has become known as the quintessential American drink. Coca-Cola's strongest competitor is Pepsi®. There are differences between the two colas, though, and many people have a favorite. Coke has a heavier, more carbonated taste and feel, and an orange-based flavor tone beneath the vanilla and cola flavors. Pepsi is lighter and sweeter, and uses a lemon-lime flavor tone beneath its cola flavoring. Also, Coke has 47 milligrams of caffeine per 12 ounce serving, compared to Pepsi's 37 milligrams. Both have about 39 grams of sugar.

These days, there is also an enormous, worldwide Coca-Cola subculture. The Coke logo has been licensed for use on a slew of products, and there are collectors all over the world who seek out these items and often pay top dollar for them. A recent search for Coke products on eBay® returned more than 30,000 individual items.

Now answer the questions on the following page without referring back to the text:

1. What stimulant besides cocaine is found in the coca leaf?
   A. Ecstasy
   B. Caffeine
   C. Ephedrine
   D. Cola

2. About how long has Coke been around?
   A. 85 years
   B. 185 years
   C. 120 years
   D. 88 years

3. What flavors are mentioned as existing in Coke (vs. Pepsi)?
   A. Vanilla, cola, and lemon-lime
   B. Cola and vanilla
   C. Vanilla, cola, and orange
   D. Orange and cola

4. Which has more sugar: Coke or Pepsi?
   A. Coke
   B. Pepsi
   C. Both
   D. Neither

A good reader should be reading fast or very fast and have gotten at least three of the four questions correct.

Answers to Quiz: 1) B; 2) C; 3) C; 4) C

You should only worry—and plan to do something about it— if you fall in the slow or very slow range and/or missed two or more questions. Otherwise, you are probably reading as fast as you need to and retaining most of what you read.

Again, the relationship between speed and comprehension is paramount: Read too fast and you may comprehend less; reading more slowly does not necessarily mean you're not grasping the material.

What *Decreases* Reading Speed/Comprehension:

1. Reading aloud or moving your lips when you read.
2. Reading mechanically—using your finger to follow words, moving your head as you read.
3. Applying the wrong kind of reading to the material.
4. Lacking sufficient vocabulary.

There are several things you can do to improve these reading mechanics.

To Increase Your Reading Speed:

1. Focus your attention and concentration.
2. Eliminate outside distractions.
3. Provide for an uncluttered, comfortable environment.
4. Don't get hung up on single words or sentences, but do look up (in the dictionary) key words that you must understand in order to grasp an entire concept.
5. Try to grasp overall concepts rather than attempting to understand every detail.

6. If you find yourself moving your lips when you read (vocalization), practice reading with a pen or some other (nontoxic, nonsugary) object in your mouth. If it falls out while you're reading, you know you have to keep working!

7. Work on building your vocabulary. You may be reading slowly (and/or having trouble understanding what you read) because your vocabulary is insufficient for your reading level.

8. Read more…and more often. Reading is a habit that improves with practice.

9. Avoid rereading words or phrases. According to one recent study, an average student reading at 250 words per minute rereads 20 times per page. The slowest readers reread the most.

To Increase Comprehension:

1. Try to make the act of learning sequential—comprehension is built by adding new knowledge to existing knowledge.

2. Review and rethink at designated points in your reading. Test yourself to see if the importance of the material is getting through.

3. If things don't add up, discard your conclusions. Go back, reread, and try to find an alternate conclusion.

4. Summarize what you've read, rephrasing it in your notes in your own words.

Most importantly, read at the speed that's comfortable for you. Though I can read extremely fast, I choose to read novels much more slowly so I can appreciate the author's wordplay. Likewise, any material that I find particularly difficult to grasp slows me right down. I read newspapers, popular magazines, and the like very fast, seeking to grasp the information but not worrying about every detail.

Should you take some sort of speed reading course, especially if your current speed level is low?

Reading for speed has some merit—many people who are slow readers read as little as possible, simply because they find it so tedious and boring. But just reading faster is not the answer to becoming a good reader.

I can't see that such a course could particularly hurt you in any way. I can also, however, recommend that you simply keep practicing reading, which will increase your speed naturally.

Don't Remember Less...Faster

Retention is primarily a product of what you understand. It has little to do with how fast you read, how great an outline you can construct, or how many fluorescent colors you use to mark your textbooks. Reading a text, grasping the message, and remembering it are the fundamentals that make for high-level retention. Reading at a 1,000-words-per-minute clip does not necessarily mean that you have a clue as to what a text really says.

If you can read an assignment faster than anyone in class, but can't give a one sentence synopsis of what you just read, your high reading rate is inconsequential. If you (eventually) get the author's message—even if it takes you an hour or two longer than some of your friends—your time will pay off in huge dividends in class and later in life.

That's why this book concentrates only on how you as a student can increase what you retain from your reading assignments. Whether you're reading a convoluted textbook that bores even the professor to tears or a magazine article, newspaper feature, or novel, you follow a certain process to absorb what you've read, which consists of:

1. Grasping the main idea.
2. Gathering the facts.
3. Figuring out the sequence of events.
4. Drawing conclusions.

When you spend an hour reading an assignment and then can't recall what you've just read, it's usually because a link in this chain has been broken. You've skipped one of these crucial steps in your reading process, leaving your understanding of the material filled with gaps.

To increase your retention rate, you need to master each level in this chain of comprehension. Not everything you read will require that you comprehend on all four levels. Following a set of cooking directions, for example, simply requires that you discern the sequence for combining all the ingredients. Other reading will demand that you be able to compile facts, identify a thesis, and give some critical thought as to its validity.

Ms. Good Reader is not only able to perform at each level of comprehension, but also has developed an instinct: She recognizes that certain things she reads can be read just to gather facts or just to grasp the main idea. She then is able to read quickly to accomplish this goal and move on to her next assignment—or to that Steven King novel she's been dying to read.

The first chapters of this book will address these different steps and provide exercises designed to help you master each stage in the process of retaining what you read.

In the final chapters, we will look at how to read literature, how to read a math or science textbook, and how to outline so that you can easily review a text.

By the time you finish this short book, you should find that, by following the procedures I've suggested, you have significantly improved your reading comprehension.

Finding Other Textbooks

Few textbooks are written by what most of us would even remotely call professional writers. While the authors and editors might well be experts, even legends, in a particular subject, writing in jargon-free, easy-to-grasp prose is probably not their strong suit. You will occasionally be assigned a textbook that is so obtuse you aren't even sure whether to read it front to back, upside down, or inside out.

If you find a particular chapter, section, or entire textbook as tough to read as getting your baby brother to do you a favor, get to the library or a bookstore and find another book covering the same subject area that you can understand.

You might even consider asking your teacher or professor for recommendations. She will probably make your job of finding a readable text a lot easier. You may even score some brownie points for your seeming initiative (as long as you don't wonder aloud what caused her to select that torturous text in the first place!).

"Ron," I hear you grumbling, "what happened to the 'study smarter, not harder' bit? This can't possibly be a time saver. Heck, I'll bet the books don't even cover the subject in the same way, let alone follow the same sequence! I'll be stuck slogging through two books."

Possibly. But if you just don't get it, maybe it's because the author just doesn't know how to explain it. Maybe it's not your fault! Too many students have sweated, moaned, dropped classes, even changed majors because they thought they were dumb, when it's possible it's the darned textbook that's dense, not you. So instead of continuing to slog though the mire, find an expert who can actually write—they're out there—and learn what you need to. After finally gaining an understanding of the subject by reading this other text, you'll find much of the original textbook much easier to use... presuming you need it at all.

CHAPTER 2

READING WITH PURPOSE

E ven if you consider yourself "not much of a reader," you read something each and every day: a magazine article, instructions for hooking up the DVD player, telephone messages tacked on the refrigerator, notes from your latest heartthrob.

Regardless of what you are reading, you have a purpose that dictates how you are going to read it—and you read different items in different ways. You wouldn't read the DVD player instructions as you would a novel any more than you'd read a magazine article in the same way as a grocery list. Without a purpose, you'd find yourself reading aimlessly and very inefficiently.

Unfortunately, many of the students I've talked to have not yet realized the importance of having a purpose for reading. Their lack of a reading purpose can be summed up by the proverb, "If you aim at nothing, you will hit the bull's-eye every time."

Before you can understand what you're reading—and remember it—you must know why you're reading it in the first place.

Defining Your Purpose for Reading

What is your purpose for reading? If the best answer you can come up with is, "Because my teacher said I had to," we need to uncover some better reasons. Reading a chapter just so you can say, "I finished my assignment" is relatively futile. You may as well put the book under a pillow and hope to absorb it by osmosis.

Unless you identify some purpose for reading, you will find yourself flipping the pages of your textbooks while seldom retaining anything more than the chapter titles.

According to reading experts, there are six fundamental purposes for reading:

1. To grasp a certain message.
2. To find important details.
3. To answer a specific question.
4. To evaluate what you are reading.
5. To apply what you are reading.
6. To be entertained.

Because reading with purpose is the first step toward improved comprehension, let me suggest some simple techniques you can use to identify a purpose for your textbook reading.

Find the Clues in Every Book

There is a group of special sections found in nearly all textbooks and technical materials (in fact, in almost all books except novels) that contain a wealth of information and can help you glean more from your reading. Becoming familiar with this data will enrich your reading experience and often make it easier. Here's what to look for.

The first page after the title page is usually the table of contents—a chapter-by-chapter list of the book's contents. Some are surprisingly detailed, listing every major point or topic covered in each chapter.

The first prose section (after the title page, table of contents, and, perhaps, an acknowledgments page), is the preface—a description of the information you will find in the book. Authors may also use the preface to point out unique aspects of their books.

The introduction may be in place of or in addition to the preface, written by the author or by some "name" the author has recruited to lend additional prestige to his or her work. Most introductions are an even more detailed overview of the book—chapter-by-chapter summaries are often included to give the reader a feel for the material to be covered.

Footnotes may be found throughout the text (a slightly elevated number following a sentence, quotation, or paragraph, e.g., "jim-dandy"[24]) and either explained at the bottom of the page on which they appear or in a special section at the back of the text. Footnotes may be used to cite sources of direct quotes or ideas and/or to further explain a point or add information outside of the text. You may make it a habit to ferret out sources cited for further reading.

If a text tends to use an alarmingly large number of terms with which you may not be familiar, the considerate author will include a glossary—essentially an abridged dictionary that defines all such terms.

The bibliography, usually at the end of the book, may include the source material the author used to research the textbook, a list of "recommended reading," or both. It is usually organized alphabetically by subject, making it easy for you to find more information on a specific topic.

Appendices containing supplementary data or examples relating to subject matter covered in the text may also appear in the back of the book.

The last thing in a book is usually the index, an alphabetical listing that references, by page number, every mention of a particular name, subject, and topic in the text.

Making it a habit to utilize all of these tools in your textbook can only make your studying easier.

Look for the Clues in Each Chapter

Every textbook offers some clues that will help you define a purpose for reading. Begin with a very quick overview of the assignment, looking for questions that you'd like answered. Consider the following elements of your reading assignment before you begin your reading.

Much like the headlines of a newspaper clue you into what the story is about, these elements will give insight into what the section or chapter is trying to communicate.

Chapter Heads and Subheads

Chapter titles and bold-faced subheads announce the detail about the main topic. And, in some textbooks, paragraph headings or bold-faced "lead-ins" announce that the author is about to provide finer details.

So start each reading assignment by going through the chapter, beginning to end, reading only the bold-faced heads and subheads.

For example, suppose you encountered the heading "The Fall of Communism" in your history textbook. You might use it to formulate the following questions:

1. *What* caused the fall of Communism?
2. *Who* caused it?
3. *When* did it fall?
4. *Why* did it fall?
5. *Where* did the fall occur?

As you read the chapter, you'll find yourself seeking answers to these questions. You now have a purpose!

Often you may find headings that contain words or terms you don't recognize. Seeking to define these terms or explain a concept should then define your purpose.

This process of headline reading takes only a few minutes, but it lays the groundwork for a more intelligent and efficient reading of the chapter. You'll have some idea of where the author is headed, which will give you a greater sense of what the most important details are and clarify where you should be concentrating your studying.

End-of-Chapter Summaries

If you read a mystery from start to finish, the way the author hopes you will, you're likely to get thrown off the scent by "red herrings" and other common detective novel devices. However, if you read the last page first, knowing the out-come will help you detect how the author constructed the novel and built an open-and-shut case for her master sleuth. You'd perceive a wealth of details about the eventually unmasked murderer that might have gone unnoticed had he been just another of the leading suspects.

Similarly, knowing what the author is driving at in a textbook will help you look for the important building blocks for his conclusions while you're reading.

It may not be fun to read a mystery novel this way, but when it comes to your textbooks, it will help you define your purpose for reading. And further, it will transform you into a much more active reader, making it less likely you'll doze off between the fall of Rome and the Black Plague.

Pictures, Graphs, and Charts

Most textbooks, particularly those in the sciences, will have charts, graphs, numerical tables, maps, and other illustrations. All too many students see these as fillers— padding to glance at and, just as quickly, forget.

If you're giving these charts and graphs short shrift, you're really shortchanging yourself. Be sure to observe how they supplement the text, what points they emphasize, and make note of these.

Highlighted Terms, Vocabulary, and Other Facts

In some textbooks, you'll discover that key terms and information are highlighted within the body text. (I don't mean highlighted by a previous student—consider such yellow-markered passages with caution!) To find the definitions of these terms or to find the application of facts may then be your purpose for reading.

Questions

Some textbook publishers use a format in which key points are emphasized by questions, either within the body or at the end of the chapter. If you read these questions before reading the chapter, you'll have a better idea of the material you should concentrate on.

If you begin your reading assignment by seeking out these heads, subheads, and other purpose-finding elements of the chapter, you'll have completed your prereading step. What is prereading? It is simply beginning your assigned reading by reviewing these clues and defining your purpose (or purposes) for reading.

I advise that you always preread every assignment! Why? Have you ever spent the better part of an evening plowing through an assignment only to finish with little or no understanding of what you just read? If the answer is yes, then you probably failed to preread it.

Reading Faster Without Speed Reading

While the heads, subheads, first sentences, and other author-provided hints we've talked about will help you get a quick read on what a chapter's about, some of the words in that chapter will help you concentrate on the important points and ignore the unimportant. Knowing when to speed up, slow down, ignore, or really concentrate will help you read both faster and more effectively.

When you see words such as "likewise," "in addition," "moreover," "furthermore," and the like, you should know that nothing new is being introduced. If you already know what's going on, speed up or skip what's coming entirely.

On the other hand, when you see words such as "on the other hand," "nevertheless," "however," "rather," "but," and their ilk, slow down—you're getting information that adds a new perspective or contradicts what you've just read.

Lastly, watch out for "payoff" words such as "to summarize," "in conclusion," "therefore," "consequently," "thus"— especially if you only have time to "hit the high points" of a chapter or you're reviewing for a test. Here's where the real meat is, where everything that went before is happily tied up in a nice bow and ribbon, a present that enables you to avoid having to unwrap the entire chapter.

Purpose Defines Reading Method

Typically, your purpose for reading dictates how you read. There are basically three types of reading we all do:

1. Quick reference reading focuses on seeking specific information that addresses a particular question or concern we might have.

2. Critical reading involves discerning ideas and concepts that require a thorough analysis.

3. Aesthetic, or pleasure reading, is what we do for sheer entertainment or to appreciate an author's style and ability.

As you define your purpose for reading, you will determine which method of reading is necessary to accomplish this purpose. In the following table are some examples of types of reading, why you might read them, and the method you should use:

Type	Purpose	Method
Newspaper advertisement	To locate best price for car	Quick reference
Magazine	To stay aware of current events	Quick reference
Self-help book	To learn to get along better with your family	Critical
Biology text	To prepare for an exam	Critical
New issue of *Rolling Stone*	To take your mind off biology!	Pleasure

If you're a good reader or desire to be one, you will always fit your reading method to your reading purpose; you have trained or are training yourself in a variety of reading skills; you have no problem switching your method to accommodate your purpose; and you are unsatisfied reading only one type of material.

A poor reader, on the other hand, reads everything the same way—doggedly plowing through his biology assignment, the newspaper, and a Stephen King novel…word by painful word. Reading with purpose is both foreign and foreboding to such a person, which makes it difficult for him to adapt a method of reading.

Become an Active Reader

Reading with purpose is as vital to your comprehension and retention as oxygen is to life. It is the cornerstone of active reading, reading that involves thinking—that process of engaging your mind and emotions in what the author is trying to communicate. Too many readers seek to absorb information passively as their eyes move across the page. The active reader involves him- or herself in receiving a message—a fact, an idea, an opinion—that is readily retained because he or she had a purpose.

Following are two passages. The first is adapted from *American Firsts* by Stephen Spignesi. The second is an excerpt from *Get Rich Slow* by Tama McAleese (Career Press, 2004). Preread each passage in order to determine a purpose for reading. Be sure to use the notes page following the passages to jot down questions that may have been raised through your preread, as well as your purpose.

Passage One

The polygraph (or "lie detector") measures physiological responses to questioning. Through various sensors and cuffs, the machine measures marked changes in blood pressure, heart rate, respiration, and perspiration, and interprets these changes to indicate that the person is being deceptive. The polygraph examiner, by law, cannot state that a person is lying. He or she can only report "Deception indicated," "No deception indicated," or "Inconclusive" for each of the examinee's responses.

The United States Supreme Court has ruled that polygraph results are inadmissible in court, writing, "there is simply no consensus that polygraph evidence is reliable…scientific field studies suggest the accuracy rate of the 'control question technique' polygraph is 'little better than could be obtained by the toss of a coin,' that is, 50 percent."

Some employers require a potential employee to submit to a lie detector test before being hired. Many job applicants do not know that they can legally decline to take the test and that they cannot be refused a job based on their unwillingness to take it. Many employees are also not aware that they can legally refuse to take a lie detector test, and that their employer cannot subsequently fire them. The only legally valid reason for an employer to demand a lie detector test of an employee is when there has been some type of embezzlement or other financial loss to the business, and the employer has reason to believe that the targeted employee was involved in the loss.

The reason polygraph results are not accepted in court is because polygraphs do not record lies; they record physical changes. Consider this scenario: You work for a company at which a computer was recently stolen from your department. You happened to see who stole it, but you had nothing to do with it, and the thief doesn't even know he was spotted. Your boss decides to polygraph everyone in the department, and when you are asked the question, "Did you steal the computer?" your blood pressure and pulse skyrocket because you do know who stole it. You answer "no" because you didn't steal it, but your body responds as if you did. In this scenario, the polygraph examiner would probably tell your boss that you were being deceptive when asked about the theft of the computer.

Your boss will probably then either fire you or make you submit to another polygraph test, which will likely turn out the same way, and then he'll fire you. You will have been branded a thief and lost your job simply because you got nervous about being asked a question about a stolen computer.

Is this fair? Of course not, and that is why polygraph results are not accepted in court.

There are books and websites devoted to teaching people how to beat a lie detector test. Some common tactics include taking a sedative before the test, placing a tack in your shoe and then stepping on it after each question, and placing deodorant on your fingertips. I have also heard of people who lie in response to every question—even "control" questions like their name, address, or gender—so the examiner cannot get a base response reading.

John Larson's invention has been the source of endless controversy, and much of the ongoing debate has been about whether or not Larson's basic postulate—that people get nervous when they lie—is true. As we all know, some people are incredibly convincing liars. They can tell you that the sky is green so persuasively that they have you looking up to confirm it's still blue.

Individuals' responses to being questioned are diverse and unpredictable. This unavoidable fact is why the Supreme Court has (wisely) rejected allowing polygraph results as valid evidence in trials.

The federal government must find ways of keeping the country expanding and workers employed. The nation's economic health is closely tied to new housing construction and existing housing sales. So Uncle Sam also has a vested interest in encouraging you to purchase the American dream.

The building industry uses the real estate industry as a middleman to turn over its housing inventory. This feeds the banking industry, which then turns to the government for guaranteed backing (something the government gets from us by selling home mortgages to investors). The insurance agent, the furniture store vendor, the county tax assessor, and the landscaper are just a few of the businesses that benefit when you commit to a home mortgage.

Homeowners are pitched so-called benefits from mortgage interest tax deductions, tax deferrals on profits from the price appreciation of their house over time, VA (Veterans Administration) and FHA (Federal Housing Authority) federally subsidized mortgage loan programs for homebuyers with little down payment. GNMA (Government National Mortgage Association, or "Ginnie Mae"), FNMA (Federal National Mortgage Association, or "Fannie Mae"), and FMAC (Federal Agricultural Mortgage Corporation, or "Farmer Mac") are lenders willing to guarantee mortgage funds back to the original lender should a homeowner default. Community rehab loans and a plump $250,000 profit per-person tax-free exclusion every two years if the house sold is your primary residence usually clinches the home sale. The homebuying industry has an

Passage Two

Ask most real estate agents, brokers, or len
tutions when the best time to buy a house is
response will usually be, "Now." If interest
low, buy before they go up. If rates are soa
now before they go higher. Can't afford a re
down payment? That's what creative financin
mortgage insurance (PMI), jumbo mortga
government subsidies are for. Don't know l
you will stay in an area? Buy that house now a
your profits when you move, or keep it ar
out for a steady monthly income. Haven't sa
reasonable down payment? Lenders will loan y
Can't fit the hefty monthly payments into you
Then spread them out over a 30-year indent
vant plan, which will give you lower paymer
with a life sentence of payments. Thinking ab
ing for a while first? You're throwing money d
drain. You don't get anything back when y
Look at all the equity that you could be build
a home instead of making a landlord rich.

The real estate industry makes its money by
real estate around from seller to buyer. It prof
pitching the advantages of home-buying. Wher
is deposited into a bank, it must be loaned out
as possible. What can the average American
a big chunk of loaned money? He or she can l
estate. So, the lender benefits by extolling the
of home ownership.

expensive and powerful agenda designed to keep its bottom line healthy. You often hear the attractive spiel: With a home, you have status; an inflation hedge; tax deductions; tax-sheltered growth; a sound, low-risk investment; increased home value through improvements; a safe investment over time; easy purchase plans; U.S. government assistance; marketability; the pride of ownership; greater family privacy; control over the roof over your head; and a proper environment to raise a family. After all, this is the American way.

But compare real estate to a bank CD as an alternative investment. Can you sell your home as fast as you can cash in a CD? Does a personal residence generate monthly or quarterly income, or any other type of guaranteed interest? Can you purchase a home as cheaply as a CD? Is the principal in your home guaranteed like the backing behind a bank CD?

There are greater risks to owning real estate than meets the eye. What about liquidity? Are you guaranteed a return on every dollar you sink into your home at sale time? The costs associated with buying and selling, and improvements and maintenance over time must be subtracted from any ultimate profits.

What if your house loses value because markets decline? Real estate doesn't always go up in price. Some homeowners have suffered major losses by buying at the top of their regional property markets. Profits they were depending on never materialized.

A CD is protected from loss of principal by an agency of the U.S. government. Can you move at a moment's notice like you can redeem your bank CD? When you rent, you are bound to stay only under the terms of your lease. The most you could lose is generally your security deposit. Do you need a job, good credit, a mortgage loan, and the promise of continued employment to buy a CD like you do to buy a house? The costs of borrowed money over the life of the mortgage are not even whispered in hallowed mortgage departments.

Can your real estate keep pace with the return on a bank CD? Probably not. On a conventional 20-year loan, you will fork over twice the amount of loan you borrowed. Over 30 years, you will pay back nearly three times the original debt. A home would have to double in price every 20 years just to keep up with that cost alone. For a 30-year loan, you would have to net three times the price you paid.

The average home cannot keep pace with a bank CD when you include the costs of ownership. Even if your home appreciates handsomely over time, there are other expenses to consider. You don't have to buy fire or theft insurance for your CD, pay property taxes or assessments or buying and selling costs, make improvements, bring your CD up to code, worry about its safety during tornado or hurricane season, or spend more money to maintain it.

Your home may be the priciest purchase you ever make. But generally it won't be listed among the top-10 smartest investments. It may even rank as one of the worst. Think of a home as a roof over your head, a place to hang your hat, and a lifestyle decision, and not as a shrewd financial investment.

Your Notes

What clues did you find that helped you define a purpose for reading each passage?

_____
_____
_____
_____
_____
_____
_____
_____

What purpose or purposes did you determine for reading each passage?

_____
_____
_____
_____
_____
_____
_____
_____

What method, based on your purpose, did you use to read each passage?

_____
_____
_____
_____
_____
_____
_____
_____

Chapter 3

Finding the Main Idea

I n all good writing there is a controlling thesis or message that connects all of the specific details and facts. This concept or idea is usually expressed as a generalization that summarizes the entire text.

Good comprehension results when you are able to grasp this main message, even if you sometimes forget some of the details. When you understand the intent, you have a context in which to evaluate the reasoning, the attitude, and whether the evidence cited really is supportive of the conclusions drawn.

An obsession for facts can obscure the "big picture," giving you an understanding of the trees but no concept of the forest. How many of you have spent hours studying for an important exam, collecting dates, names, terms, and formulas, but failed to ferret out the main idea, the underlying concept that is composed of these facts?

In longer, more involved readings, many messages are combined to form a chain of thought, which, in turn, may or may not communicate one thesis or idea.

Your ability to capture this chain of thought determines your level of comprehension—and what you retain.

Dissecting Your Reading Assignment

To succeed in identifying the main idea in any reading assignment, you must learn to use these helpful tools:

1. The topic sentence of a paragraph.

2. Summary sentences.

3. Supporting sentences.

4. Transitional statements.

As you learn to dissect your reading assignment paragraph by paragraph, identifying its many parts and their functions, you'll grasp the main idea much more quickly—and remember it much longer.

Recognizing a Topic Sentence

Every paragraph has a topic sentence—the sentence that summarizes what the paragraph is about. Even if a paragraph does not have such a clearly stated sentence, it can be implied or inferred from what is written.

Generally, the topic sentence is the first or last sentence of a paragraph—the one statement that announces, "Here's what this paragraph is all about!"

When the topic sentence is obscured or hidden, you may need to utilize two simple exercises to uncover it:

1. Pretend you're a headline writer for your local newspaper and write a headline for the paragraph you just read.

2. Write a five-word summary describing what the paragraph is about.

Exercise: Identifying a Topic Sentence

Write a headline or five-word summary for each of the following paragraphs:

Mary Phelps Jacob invented the brassiere when she needed something to wear beneath a gown and none of the existing undergarments of the time gave her the support the garment required. Women wore corsets back then, and they were bulky, uncomfortable, and did not work for many types of dresses. In Mary's case, the sheer gown she had bought had a plunging neckline and the whalebone inserts of her corsets were visible. After a little thought, Mary designed the first bra using nothing but two silk handkerchiefs and some pink ribbon. She fashioned two cups out of the handkerchiefs, used the ribbon to tie them and, voila, no more corsets!

Jazz is a musical feast, and its recipe includes African-American gospel spirituals, blues, ragtime, and other musical forms popularized and remade by American musicians. The earliest pioneers of jazz were the New Orleans Dixieland musicians who taught themselves to play, but who could not read or write music. They would turn beloved old favorites like "When the Saints Come Marching In" and "The Battle Hymn of the Republic" into rollicking, freeform musical epics.

Early versions of sewing machines were created in England and France, but they were completely unworkable as commercial machines. Thomas Saint's machine, for example, designed in 1790 to sew leather, was never even built. Barthelmy Thimonnier invented a machine in France in the late 1820s that sewed a chain stitch using a crocheting needle. He enjoyed some success with the machine sewing soldier's uniforms for the French Army, but his shop and machines were destroyed by rampaging tailors who believed that Thimonnier was set on putting them out of business and that any machines designed to replace human labor were sinful.

You can begin your analysis by turning, once again, to our helpful questions. Is the passage written to address one of the questions?

1. **Who?** The paragraph focuses on a particular person or group of people. The topic sentence tells you who this is.

2. **When?** The paragraph is primarily concerned with time. The topic sentence may even begin with the word "when."

3. **Where?** The paragraph is oriented around a particular place or location. The topic sentence states where you are reading about.

4. **Why?** A paragraph that states reasons for some belief or happening usually addresses this question. The topic sentence answers why something is true or why an event happened.

5. **How?** The paragraph identifies the way something works or the means by which something is done. The topic sentence explains the how of what is described.

You will notice that I didn't include the question "What?" in this list. This is not an oversight. "What?" addresses such a broad range of possibilities that asking this question will not necessarily lead you to the topic sentence.

The best test to determine whether you have identified the topic sentence is to rephrase it as a question. If the paragraph answers the question that you've framed, you've found the topic sentence.

Summary, Support, or Transitional?

Another technique that will lead you to the topic sentence is to identify what purpose other sentences in the paragraph serve—kind of a process of elimination.

Generally, sentences can be characterized as summary, support, or transitional.

Summary sentences state a general idea or concept. As a rule, a topic sentence is a summary sentence—a concise yet inclusive statement that expresses the general intent of the paragraph. (By definition, the topic sentence is never a support sentence.)

Support sentences provide the specific details and facts that give credibility to the author's points of view. They give examples, explain arguments, offer evidence, or attempt to prove something as true or false. They are not meant to state generally what the author wants to communicate—they are intended to be specific, not conceptual, in nature.

Transitional sentences move the author from one point to another. They may be viewed as bridges connecting the paragraphs in a text, suggesting the relationship between what you just finished reading and what you are about to read. Good readers are attuned to the signals such sentences provide—they are buzzers that scream, "This is what you are going to find out next!"

Transitional sentences may also alert you to what you should have just learned. Unlike support sentences, transitional sentences provide invaluable and direct clues to identifying the topic sentence.

Some Examples of Transitional Signals

Any sentence that continues a progression of thought or succession of concepts is a transitional sentence. Such a sentence may begin with a word such as "first," "next," "finally," or "then," and indicate the before/after connection between changes, improvements, or alterations.

Transitional sentences that begin in this way should raise these questions in your mind:

1. Do I know what the previous examples were?
2. What additional example am I about to learn?
3. What was the situation prior to the change?

Other transition statements suggest a change in argument or thought or an exception to a rule. These will generally be introduced by words like "but," "although," "though," "rather," "however," or similar conjunctions that suggest an opposing thought.

Such words ought to raise these questions:

1. What is the gist of the argument I just read?
2. What will the argument I am about to read state?
3. To what rule is the author offering an exception?

In your effort to improve your reading, developing the ability to recognize the contrast between general, inclusive words and statements (summary sentences) and specific, detail-oriented sentences (transitional or support sentences) is paramount.

Taking Notes

The final step toward grasping and retaining the main idea of any paragraph is taking notes. There are several traditional methods students employ—outlining, highlighting, mapping, and drawing concept trees.

An exhaustive review of all these methods is not within the scope of this particular book, but for a complete discussion of note-taking techniques, be sure to read *Get Organized*, another of the books in my *How to Study Program*.

Whichever method you employ to retain the main idea, focus on the topic sentences, not on the specific details.

If you are a highlighter—you enjoy coloring textbooks with fluorescent markers—you will want to assign one color that you will always use to highlight topic sentences. Avoid what too many students do—highlighting virtually every paragraph. This practice will just extend your review time considerably—you'll find yourself rereading instead of reviewing.

If you utilize outlining or mapping (diagramming what you read rather than spending time worrying about Roman numerals and whether to use lowercase letters or uppercase letters on certain lines), you will find that your time will best be spent writing five-word summaries of the topic sentences.

If you find yourself getting bogged down in details and specifics, you are wasting valuable time. Again, writers are using these details to communicate their concepts—they are not necessarily to be remembered.

Read the following passages, seeking out the topic sentences. Then summarize the main idea or ideas in five-word phrases. (The first two are adapted from *American Firsts* by Stephen Spignesi, which, as you probably have guessed, is a favorite of mine; the last from *Why Women Earn Less* by Mikelann R. Valterra [Career Press, 2004].)

Passage One

American Alexander Graham Bell did not invent the telephone; Italian-American Antonio Meucci did. On June 15, 2002, the United States Congress officially recognized Meucci as the true inventor of the telephone. Many of you may know that Bell received the patent for a telephonic device mere hours before a patent for a similar device by an inventor named Elisha Gray was filed. What many of you probably do not know is that it has now been proven that Bell probably stole the idea for the telephone from designs and drawings by Antonio Meucci that were stored in the laboratory where Bell worked. The United States Supreme Court annulled Bell's patent in 1887 on the grounds of fraud and misrepresentation.

The telephone patent is considered today to be the most valuable patent ever issued by the U.S. government. Meucci was born in Florence, Italy, in 1807 and emigrated to America in 1845. Between 1850 and 1862, Meucci developed at least 30 different models of working telephones. (The German inventor Philip Reis, who has sometimes also been credited as being the true inventor of the telephone, invented a voice-transmitting device in 1861, more than a decade after Meucci's earliest models.)

However, Meucci was too poor to pay the fees required to patent his inventions (around $250), and he had to settle for a document called a Caveat, which was a formal legal notice that stated that he had invented the telephone. The caveat was meant to be temporary until official patent papers could be acquired, but Meucci did not even have the money to renew the caveat. In 1874, he turned over some of his models to the vice president of Western Union Telegraphs, and, two years later, read in the newspaper that Alexander Graham Bell (who, remember, had been working at the Western Union Labs), had patented a telephone and taken full credit for its invention. Even though this patent was annulled, Meucci never profited from his invention and he died poor in 1889.

Passage Two

Rituals have arisen surrounding the game of Monopoly. Some people will only play if they are the thimble, or the top hat. Some will only target certain properties to purchase. Some will take a drink every time they pay rent. And then there's naked Monopoly...but we won't go there.

Monopoly is the world's best-selling board game. Yes, in this age of computer and video games and astonishingly high-tech handheld games, the defiantly low-tech Monopoly is still the king. Who invented the game of Monopoly? History accepts Charles Darrow as the inventor because he was the one who went to Parker Brothers with the idea, he was the one from whom they bought the rights, and he was the one who became a millionaire from Monopoly royalties.

However, there is compelling evidence that Darrow was taught the game by a woman who had been playing something she had invented, called The Landlord's Game, for years. The Landlord's Game was very similar to today's Monopoly except that the goal was not to acquire property, but rather to denigrate property ownership and landlords.

The story told by those in the Darrow camp is that Darrow came up with the idea for Monopoly when he was unemployed during the Great Depression. He nostalgically sketched out the streets of his childhood hometown of Atlantic City, New Jersey, and eventually developed the idea of buying and selling property as the "play" of the game. Supposedly, his friends and neighbors loved the game and would spend evenings playing it at the Darrow home. Darrow began making copies of the game board and rules and selling them for four dollars apiece. He also began offering it to stores in Philadelphia.

The game's burgeoning popularity spurred Darrow to offer it to Parker Brothers, who turned it down because it took too long to play and because they said it was too complicated.

Darrow was not discouraged, though, and continued to market the game on his own.

How did it eventually end up a Parker Brothers game after Parker Brothers rejected it? A friend of one of George Parker's daughters bought one of Darrow's games and recommended it to Parker's daughter Sally. This time, Parker Brothers sought out Darrow and bought the rights to the game.

This story is the "official" version. There have been several lawsuits, however, regarding the true genesis of the game, and Parker Brothers has paid out cash settlements to people who have shown that Darrow likely did not create Monopoly on his own.

Passage Three

Many women chronically earn less than they could, and are tired and frustrated at their apparent inability to increase their earnings. This pattern of not making enough money is called "underearning," and is a tragic waste of potential and possibility in the lives of thousands of women. Underearning happens when you repeatedly (and consistently) make less than you need or than would be helpful to you, usually despite your desire to make more money. Put another way: An underearner is someone who doesn't get paid as much as might be expected, given her experience, education, and training.

Underearning takes on many forms and can be as creative and varied as the underearner. Those on a salary may have a hard time asking for that long over-due raise, while those who are self-employed might find it difficult to raise their fees. Sometimes people give their time away by under-billing. Others under-earn by using all their energy for volunteer activities, and in the process give away their skills and experience. And some people underearn by failing to market them-selves, whether or not they are self-employed.

Some of these practices are part of everyday life, and are so common that most women do not understand how their behavior limits their earning potential. Also, underearning can result from what one doesn't do, which makes it more easily unnoticed, ignored, or forgotten. But the end result is the same: when women undersell themselves, the price they pay is very high. Millions of women underearn—yet have no idea they are doing so.

During the course of a working lifetime, this chronic underselling results in the loss of what most of us would consider a small fortune. In fact, current research shows that the average 25-year-old woman will earn $523,000 less than her male counterpart over the next 40 years, according to the Institute of Women's Policy Research. Imagine—more than half a million dollars lost, never to be recouped! That's the bad news. The good news is that many of the causes of underearning can be eliminated, and you have the power to make that happen, though you may not yet realize it.

It is possible to make more money. But in order to do so, you must first learn how to recognize your own underearning, and to understand the issues that motivate your behavior. Only then can you develop a solid, workable plan to reverse the pattern of selling yourself short.

So how did you do taking notes on these three examples? I didn't always keep my summaries to five words, but I distilled the main ideas to the fewest words I could.

Nor did I always write one summary statement per paragraph—just what was needed to capture the main idea or ideas from each paragraph.

CHAPTER 4

GATHERING THE FACTS

"Now, what I want is facts. Teach these boys and girls nothing but facts.
Facts alone are wanted in life. Plant nothing else, and root out
everything else. You can only form the minds of reasoning animals
upon facts: nothing else will ever be of any service to them.
This is the principle on which I bring up my own children,
and this is the principle on which I bring up these children.
Stick to facts, sir!"

—Charles Dickens, *Hard Times*

While such an approach is not the only ingredient for scholastic success, you'll find that the vast majority of your assigned reading requires a thorough recall of the facts.

In the previous chapter, we discussed the "forest"—the main idea. In this chapter, we will concentrate on "the trees"— how to read to gather facts, the specific details that support and develop the author's main point.

Facts: Building Blocks for Ideas

Facts are the building blocks that give credibility to concepts and ideas. Your ability to gather and assimilate these facts will dramatically enhance your success at remembering what the author wanted to communicate.

If, however, you spend so much time studying the trees that you lose sight of the forest, your reading effectiveness will be limited. You must learn to discern what facts are salient to your understanding, and which ones to leave for the next Trivial Pursuit update.

If you are trying to identify your purpose for reading this chapter, it's threefold:

1. To develop the skill of scanning a text for facts as quickly as possible.

2. To distinguish between an important detail and a trivial one.

3. To learn how to skim text—reading and absorbing its essence, even when you're not looking for anything in particular.

Deciphering the Message

The author of any kind of writing should have something to say, a message to communicate.

Unfortunately, such messages are often lost in the glut of verbiage many authors use to "dress up" their basic point. It's your job to rake through the mess and get to the heart of the text.

You need to approach each reading assignment with the mindset of Sherlock Holmes: There is a mystery to be solved, and you are the master detective. The goal is to figure out what the text is trying to communicate—regardless of how deeply it is buried in the quagmire of convoluted language.

What Is the Message?

The first step in any good investigation is to collect all of the clues. What are the facts? By spending a few minutes of your time discerning these concrete facts, you will be far better equipped to digest what it is the author is trying to communicate.

But how do you extract the facts when they appear to be hidden in an impenetrable forest of words? You may need a little help—from "who-what-when-where-why-and-how." It seems that the facts readily sally forth when these six trusty questions are called upon the scene.

Exercise: Read the following excerpt (from *Homework Helpers: Biology* by Matthew Distefano, Career Press, 2004), keeping those six words in mind, then answer the questions that follow.

> The earliest development of the microscope took place a long time after people had discovered the magnifying power of lenses. A container of water, a bead of glass, or a gemstone can all magnify objects to some degree and can be considered early lenses. Roger Bacon (1214–1294) is given credit for introducing the magnifying lens as eye glasses, or spectacles, as they were known during his time, in 1268. This is probably

the first recorded time a magnifying glass was used to support human eyesight.

It would take several hundred years before these glass lenses were used to make distant objects appear closer or small objects appear bigger. The invention of the telescope was in 1608 by a Dutch lens maker named Hans Lippershey. The microscope was probably created a few years earlier, around 1597, by Zaccharias Jansseen and his son Han, who were also Dutch lens makers. This father-and-son combo created the earliest documented compound microscope by focusing light through two lenses. Robert Hooke would later refine the structure of the compound microscope.

Anton van Leeuwenhoek (1632–1723), a naturalist and lens maker, constructed a very powerful lens to view small objects. Van Leeuwenhoek created large single lens microscopes that could magnify objects up to 270X their normal size. With these lenses, he saw small objects that had never been seen by human eyes before, such as bacterial cells, protozoa, and blood and yeast cells.

Robert Hooke (1635–1703), a physicist by trade, refined the structure of the compound microscope. As mentioned earlier, a compound microscope is a microscope where the object is now viewed through two lenses, instead of just one. Hooke is credited with coining the word "cell," when he described the many small, interconnected boxes he saw under the microscope while looking at a piece of cork. Cork is made from tree bark, so it consists of dead plant cells. Hooke, although not known to him at the time, was viewing these dead plant cells.

In 1831, Robert Brown, a botanist, was the first to describe the dark, circular object found at the center of all plant cells as a nucleus.

In 1838, Matthias Schleiden, a botanist, and Theodor Schwann, a zoologist, concluded that all living things are made of cells, and in 1855, Rudolph Virchow added that all cells arise only from other living cells. The work of these three scientists led to what is today known as the cell theory.

Questions

1. Who first described the nucleus?
   A. Rudolph Virchow
   B. Matthias Schleiden
   C. Theodor Schwann
   D. None of the above

2. About how many times could van Leeuwenhoek's lens magnify objects?
   A. 10
   B. 100
   C. 200
   D. 300

3. In what century was the microscope probably invented?
   A. 15th
   B. 16th
   C. 17th
   D. 18th

4. In what century was the magnifying lens first used in eyeglasses?

A. 12th

B. 13th

C. 15th

D. 17th

5. Who invented the telescope?

A. Robert Brown

B. Anton van Leeuwenhoek

C. Robert Hooke

D. Hans Lippershey

In the preceding exercise, you should have quickly read through the text and been able to answer all five questions. If it took you more than three minutes to do so, you spent too much time. You were reading only to answer "who?", "what?", "when?", "where?", "why?", and "how?" Your purpose was to get to the facts, nothing more.

Scanning, Skimming, Reading, Remembering

Most everyone I know confuses skim and scan. Let me set the record straight. Skim is to read quickly and superficially. Scan is to read carefully but for a specific item. So when you skim a reading selection, you are reading it in its entirety, though you're only hitting the "highlights."

When you scan a selection, you are reading it in detail but only until you find what you're looking for. Scanning is the technique we all employ when using the phone book—unless, of course, you're in the habit of reading every name in the book to find the one you're looking for. When you scan, your eyes do not look at every word, read every sentence, or think about every paragraph. Instead, they rapidly move across the page to find just what you are looking for and then read that carefully.

Scanning is the fastest reading rate of all—although you are reading in detail, you are not seeking to comprehend or remember anything that you see until you find the bit of information you're looking for.

When I was in college, I would begin any assignment by reading the first sentence of every paragraph and trying to answer the questions at the chapter's end. If this did not give me a pretty good idea of the content and important details of that chapter, then—and only then—would I read it more thoroughly.

I'm sure this method of skimming for the facts saved me countless hours of time (and boredom).

Ask First, Then Look

When skimming for detail, you will often have a particular question, date, or fact to find. You should approach the text much like the dictionary—knowing the word, you just scan the pages to find its definition. If you must answer a specific question or read about a historic figure, you simply find a source—book, magazine, encyclopedia, or website—and quickly scan the text for the answer or person.

You probably are assigned a lot of reading that can be accomplished by skimming for facts. By establishing the questions you want answered before you begin to read, you can quickly browse through the material, extracting only the information you need.

Let's say you're reading a science book with the goal of identifying the function of a cell's nucleus. You can breeze through the section that gives the parts of the cell. You can skim the description of what cells do. You already know what you're looking for—and there it is in the section that talks about what each cell part does. Now you can start to read.

By identifying the questions you wanted to answer (a.k.a. your purpose) in advance, you would be able to skim the chapter and answer your questions in a lot less time than it would have taken to painstakingly read every word.

As a general rule, if you are reading textbook material word for word, you probably are wasting quite a bit of your study time. Good readers are able to discern what they should read in this manner and what they can afford to skim. When trying to simply gather detail and facts, skimming a text is a simple and very important shortcut.

Alternatively, your ability to skim a chapter—even something you need to read more critically—will enable you to develop a general sense of what the chapter is about and how thoroughly it needs to be read.

Exercise: Answer the following questions by skimming the paragraph that follows:

1. How many miles of coastline does Brazil have?

2. Which two South American countries do not border Brazil?

3. Which river is Brazil home to?

> The largest country in South America is also the fifth largest country in the world. The Republic of Brazil is a vast land covering more than 3.3 million square miles—nearly half of the continent—with 4,600 miles of coastline looking out into the Atlantic Ocean. Brazil borders every country in South America except for Chile and Ecuador. This huge nation is home to a variety of climates and natural attractions, including immense rainforests and the world's largest river, the Amazon.

If this were part of your assigned reading, you would be finished when you had answered the questions. "But I didn't read it," you protest. Can you write a one-sentence summary of the paragraph? If you can, and you answered the questions correctly, then you know all you need to.

Skimming, or prereading, is a valuable step even if you aren't seeking specific facts. When skimming for a general overview, there's a very simple procedure to follow:

1. If there is a title or heading, rephrase it as a question. This will be your purpose for reading.

2. Examine all the subheadings, illustrations, and graphics, as these will help you identify the significant matter within the text.

3. Read thoroughly the introductory paragraphs, the summary, and any questions at the chapter's end.

4. Read the first sentence of every paragraph. As we found in Chapter 3, this is generally where the main idea of a text is found.

5. Evaluate what you have gained from this process: Can you answer the questions at the end of the chapter? Could you intelligently participate in a class discussion of the material?

6. Write a brief summary that encapsulates what you have learned from your skimming.

7. Based on this evaluation, decide whether a more thorough reading is required.

Exercise: Let's see how well you can skim for an overview, rather than for specific facts. Read the following two passages, then follow the seven steps outlined previously for each. The first is from *Hollywood Urban Legends* (New Page Books, 2001) by movie reviewer Roger Ebert's erstwhile partner, Richard Roeper. The second is from William's Weir's description of the battle of Hattin in 1187 A.D. in *50 Battles That Changed the World* (New Page Books, 2001).

Passage One

What a group of misfit castaways they truly were, from the fat guy who always thought he was in charge to the old crank to the sexy young babes to the unathletic guy who couldn't do anything right. No, I'm not talking about the first season of *Survivor*, I'm talking about *Gilligan's Island*.

Now, you might think of *G.I.* (as Tina Louise has always insisted on calling it in interviews because she can't bear to say the name "Gilligan" anymore) as nothing more than an astoundingly idiotic, stupid sitcom with no redeeming values—a brainless exercise in lamebrained humor that will play forever in Rerun Hell.

Well, you're probably right. But there are those who believe that *Gilligan's Island* is so much more complex than that. The show's creator, Sherwood Schwartz, is a learned and sophisticated man who always felt guilty about going into television, because he knew his creative genius could have been put to better use in another field, like rocket science or plastics. Deep down, Schwartz wanted to give the world TV programs that would educate us, that would tell us something about the human condition, that would elevate the human spirit—but the powers-that-be at the network level didn't want to hear that sort of nonsense. They wanted funny hits—commercially viable pap that could be used to sell dishwashing detergent and new cars to the masses. In other words, they wanted *Gilligan's Island*.

Little did the execs at CBS know that Schwartz played a trick of sorts with *Gilligan's Island* by giving it a subliminal second life that existed as a running social commentary about the state of the world. Not even the writers or cast members knew about this, but the truth is, they each represented one of the seven deadly sins!

1. Ginger, with her Marilyn Monroe voice and her plunging neckline gowns, was Lust.

2. Mary Ann, who could never be as sexy as Ginger, was Envy.

3. The Professor, who could construct a telescope from a coconut shell and bragged about knowing a little bit about everything, was Pride.

4. Mr. Howell, the millionaire, was Greed.

5. Mrs. Howell, who treated the other castaways like they were her servants and never did anything herself, was Sloth.

6. The Skipper, with his insatiable appetite, was Gluttony.

7. The Skipper was also Anger, for constantly losing his temper and hitting Gilligan with his hat.

And that leaves the deceptively benign Gilligan, who was Satan himself. *Gilligan's Island* is actually Hell! He keeps the others there through one foul-up after another. Week after week, the castaways are allowed to glimpse a ray of hope that they'll be able to get off the island, but it's all a mirage. They never realize that they're doomed to spend all eternity there—courtesy of Gilligan, who always wears red, the most devilish of colors.

Gilligan's Island as a metaphor for Hell is also Schwartz's way of admitting his own existence was hellish. Just as the castaways were trapped on that island, Schwartz was trapped in the mindless world of TV sitcoms, doomed to spend his professional life wallowing in shallow inanity. Pretty deep lagoon we're wading in, eh? Academic journals and Internet philosophers have delighted in advancing the "Seven Deadly Sins" theory of *Gilligan's Island*, and in later years, Schwartz himself has not discouraged such thought.

Passage Two

"So formidable is the charge of the Frankish cavalry with their broadsword, lance, and shield, that it is best to decline a pitched battle with them until you have put all the chances on your own side."

So advised the Byzantine emperor, Leo the Wise. Leo was thinking of the knights of the Carolingian Empire, but the techniques of Charlemagne's knights had been adopted all over Europe when the Crusades began. Still, perhaps because the first Crusaders were overwhelmingly French or Norman, to Byzantines and Muslims alike, all Westerners were "Franks." And Leo's advice was still sound.

War in Europe—a moist mass of peninsulas and islands, covered with forests and broken up by rivers and mountains—meant fighting at close quarters. Knights were encased in heavy mail, and foot soldiers wore as much armor as they could afford. Often the knight's huge charger, or destrier, was also armored. The destrier's saddle let the knight put all his weight and his horse's weight behind a lance thrust. The lance and the sword were the Western knight's only weapons, the charge his only tactic.

Horsemen of the steppes, unhampered by woods or many rivers, covered wide areas in their skirmishing. They depended mostly on the bow and usually charged only after their foes had been thoroughly softened up by archery. Asian tactics left little room for infantry, except in sieges.

The Frankish footmen, who had beaten the Romans, Goths, Vandals, Huns, and Arabs for centuries, had not forgotten how to fight. They were armed with spears, shields, and a new weapon: the recently reinvented crossbow.

Anna Comnena, a Byzantine princess, described the device she saw in the hands of the first Crusaders: "It is a weapon unknown to Greeks and to the Barbarians. This terrible weapon is not worked by drawing its cord with the right hand, and holding it with the left hand. The user rests both his feet against the bow, whilst he strains at the bow with the full force of his arms... When the cord is released, the arrow leaves the groove with a force against which nothing is proof. It not only penetrates a buckler, but also pierces the man and his armour through and through."

The Crusaders' military system was based on the close coordination of crossbowmen, infantry spearmen, and heavily armored knights. The disciplined spearmen kept the Turkish horse archers away from the knights, who led their destriers until they were ready to fight. Between every two spearmen was a crossbow-man who shot down Saracens before they could get close enough to hit anything with their bows. If the frustrated Muslims tried to break through the Christian lines with a mass attack, the infantry opened its ranks and the mounted knights charged. As at Marathon, the Westerners had heavier armor and carried longer spears. Unless there was an enormous imbalance of numbers the Muslims always lost.

While it may not be evident at first, you'll soon see how skimming can save you a lot of reading time. Even if a more in-depth reading is necessary, you will find that by having gone through this process, you will have developed the kind of skeletal framework that will make your further reading faster, easier, and more meaningful. And if all you need is "Just the facts, ma'am," your ability to scan a selection, chapter, or book will save you minutes, if not hours, every week.

Whether you're skimming or scanning, you will have equipped yourself with the ability to better digest whatever the author is trying to communicate.

CHAPTER 5

THE CHALLENGE OF TECHNICAL TEXTS

You've already learned a lot of ways to improve your reading. It's time to examine the unique challenges posed by highly technical texts. Physics, trigonometry, chemistry, calculus—you know, subjects that three-fourths of all students avoid like the plague. Even those students who manage to do well in such subjects wouldn't dare call them "Mickey Mouse" courses.

More than any other kind of reading, these subjects demand a logical, organized approach and a step-by-step reading method.

And they require a detection of the text's organizational devices.

Developing the skill to identify the basic sequence of the text will enable you to follow the progression of thought, a progression that is vital to your comprehension and retention.

Why? In most technical writing, each concept is a like a building block of understanding—if you don't understand a particular section or concept, you won't be able to understand the next section either.

Most technical books are saturated with ideas, terms, formulas, and theories. The chapters are dense with information, compressing a great wealth of ideas into a small space. They demand to be read very carefully.

In order to get as much as possible from such reading assignments, you can take advantage of some devices to make sense of the organization. Here are five basics to watch for:

1. Definitions and terms.

2. Examples.

3. Classifications and listings.

4. Comparison and contrast.

5. Cause-effect relationships.

As you read any text, but certainly a highly specialized one, identifying these devices will help you grasp the main idea, as well as any details that are essential to your thorough understanding of the material.

Definitions and Terms

In reading any specialized text, you must begin at the beginning—understanding the terms particular to that discipline. Familiar, everyday words have very precise definitions in technical writing.

What do I mean? Take the word nice. You may compliment your friend's new sweater, telling her it's nice, meaning attractive. You may find that the new chemistry teacher is nice, meaning he doesn't give too much homework. And when your friend uses the word nice to describe the blind date she's set up for you, it may mean something completely different—and insidious.

Everyday words can have a variety of meanings, some of them even contradictory, depending on the context in which they're used.

In contrast, in the sciences, terminology has fixed and specific meanings. For example, the definition of elasticity— "the ability of a solid to regain its shape after a deforming force has been applied"—is the same in Bangkok or Brooklyn. Such exact terminology enables scientists to communicate with the precision their discipline requires.

Definitions may vary in length. One term may require a one sentence definition; others merit entire paragraphs. Some may even need a whole chapter to accurately communicate the definition.

Look for key words that indicate specific mathematical operations. You need to add when you see words such as "increased by," "combined," "together," "sum," or "total of;" subtract when you see "decreased by," "minus," "less," "difference;" multiply when you see "product," "increased," "by a factor of," and "times;" and divide when you see "per," "ratio," "quotient," or "percent."

Examples

A second communication tool is the example. Authors use examples as bridges between abstract principles and concrete illustrations. These examples are essential to your ability to comprehend intricate and complicated theories.

Unlike other writing, technical writing places a very high premium on brevity. Economizing words is the key to covering a large volume of knowledge in a relatively small space. Few technical texts or articles include anecdotal matter or chatty stories on the author's experiences.

This fact challenges the reader to pay particular attention to the examples that are included. Why? Technical writing often is filled with new or foreign ideas—many of which are not readily digestible. They are difficult in part because they are abstract. Examples work to clarify these concepts, hopefully in terms that are more easily understood.

For example, it may be difficult for you to make sense of the definition of symbiosis—"the living together of two dissimilar organisms, especially when mutually beneficial"—but the example of the bird that picks food from the crocodile's teeth, thereby feeding itself and keeping the crocodile cavity-free, helps bring it home.

Classifications and Listings

A third tool frequently utilized in texts is classifications and listings. Classifying is the process by which common subjects are categorized under a general heading.

Here are two examples:

There are four seasons: winter, spring, summer, and fall.
Classification: seasons
Listing: winter, spring, summer, fall

There are four time zones in the United States: Eastern, Central, Mountain, and Pacific.
Classification: U.S. time zones
Listing: Eastern, Central, Mountain, Pacific

Especially in technical writing, authors use classification to categorize extensive lists of detail. Such writings may have several categories and subcategories that organize these details into some manageable fashion.

Comparing/Contrasting

A fourth tool used in communicating difficult information is that of comparing and contrasting. Texts use this tool to bring complicated material into focus by offering a similar or opposing picture.

Such devices are invaluable in grasping concepts that do not conjure a picture in your mind. Gravity, for example, is not something that can be readily pictured—it's not a tangible object that can be described.

Through comparison, a text relates a concept to one that has been previously defined—or to one a reader may readily understand. Through contrast, the text concentrates on the differences and distinctions between two ideas. By focusing on distinguishing features, these ideas become clearer as one idea is held up against another.

Cause-Effect Relationships

A final tool that texts employ to communicate is the cause-effect relationship. This device is best defined in the context of science, where it is the fundamental quest of most scientific research.

Science begins with the observation of the effect—what is happening? For instance, say it is snowing.

The next step is to conduct research into the cause: Why is it snowing? Detailing this cause-effect relationship is often the essence of scientific and technical writing.

Cause-effect relationships may be written in many ways. The effect may be stated first, followed by the cause. An effect may be the result of several connected causes—a causal chain. And a cause may have numerous effects.

In your reading, it is vital that you recognize this relationship and its significance.

Read with a Plan

More than any other type of writing, highly specialized technical writing must be read with a plan. You can't approach your reading assignment merely with the goal of completing it. Such mindless reading will leave you confused and frustrated, drowning in an ocean of theory, concepts, terms, and examples.

Your plan should incorporate the following guidelines:

1. Learn the terms that are essential to understanding the concepts presented. Knowing the precise definitions that the author uses will enable you to follow his chain of thought through the text.

2. Determine the structure or organization of the text. Most chapters have a definite pattern that forms the skeleton of the material. A book may begin with a statement of a theory, give examples, provide sample problems, then summarize. Often this pattern can be discerned through a preview of the table of contents or the titles and subtitles.

3. Skim the chapter to get a sense of the author's viewpoint. Ask questions to define your purpose in reading. Use any summaries or review questions to guide your reading.

4. Complete a thorough analytical reading of the text. Do not proceed from one section to the next until you have a clear understanding of the section you are reading—the concepts generally build upon each other. To proceed to a new section without understanding the ones that precede it is, at best, futile.

5. Immediately upon concluding your thorough reading, review! Write a summary of the concepts and theories you need to remember. Answer any questions raised when you skimmed the text. Do the problems. If possible, apply the formulas.

Technical material is saturated with ideas. When reading it, you must be convinced of one fact: Every individual word counts! You will want to read such material with the utmost concentration—it is not meant to be sped through.

Good readers know that such material demands a slow read that concentrates on achieving the greatest level of retention.

- Every definition has to be digested.
- Every formula must be committed to memory.
- Every example needs to be considered.

To improve your reading of such technical material, you will want to hone the skill of identifying the devices an author uses to communicate. In so doing, you will be able to connect the chain of thought that occurs. When reading such texts—or attempting to work out technical problems—try the following "tricks":

- Whenever you can, "translate" numbers and formulae into words. To test your understanding, try to put your translation into different words.
- Even if you're not particularly visual, pictures can often help. You should try translating a particularly vexing math problem into a drawing or diagram.

- Before you even get down to solving a problem, is there any way for you to estimate the answer or, at least, to estimate the range within which the answer should fall (greater than 1, but less than 10)? This is the easy way to at least make sure you wind up in the right ballpark.

- Play around. There are often different paths to the same solution, or even equally valid solutions. If you find one, try to find others. This is a great way to increase your understanding of all the principles involved.

- When you are checking your calculations, try working backwards. I've found it an easier way to catch simple mathematical errors.

- Try to figure out what is being asked, what principles are involved, what information is important, and what is not.

- Teach someone else. Trying to explain mathematical concepts to someone else will quickly pinpoint what you really know or don't know. It's virtually impossible to get someone else—especially someone who is slower than you at all this stuff—to understand if you don't!

5. If it seems that you will need several hours to complete your reading, break it into smaller, more manageable parts, then reward yourself at the end of each of these sections with a brief break.

If you take these steps prior to reading any text that requires your utmost concentration, you will find that your mind is readied for the kind of focus necessary to read critically. Make a habit of such preparations and you will set yourself up to succeed.

Prereading Is a Must

Once you have prepared your mind to read, the next step is to understand the big picture—what is the author's thesis or main idea? Good comprehension is the consequence of your ability to grasp the main point of what the author is trying to communicate.

And grasping this message is accomplished through skimming the text, as we discussed in Chapter 4. Let's review the basic steps:

1. If there is a title or heading, rephrase it as a question. This will support your purpose for reading.

2. Examine all subheadings, illustrations, and graphics, as these will help you identify the significant matter within the text.

3. Read the introductory paragraphs, summary, and any questions at the end of the chapter.

4. Read the first sentence of every paragraph. In Chapter 3 you learned that this is generally where the main idea is found.

5. Evaluate what you have gained from this process: Can you answer the questions at the chapter's end? Could you intelligently participate in a class discussion of the material?

6. Write a brief summary of what you have learned from your skimming.

Now, Read It

Once you identify and understand the basic skeleton of the material, your actual "read" of the material—following the details, reasoning, and chain of thought—is simply a matter of attaching meat to the bones.

This digestive process involves learning to interpret and evaluate what is written, what is directly stated, and what can be inferred from the context.

Effective analytical reading requires that you, the reader, distinguish the explicit, literal meaning of words (denotation) and what suggestions or intentions are intimated by the general content (connotation).

Analyzing: What the Words Connote

Words and writing have two levels of meaning that are important to the reader's comprehension.

The first level is the literal or descriptive meaning. What a word expressly denotes means the specific, precise definition you'd find in the dictionary.

Connotation involves this second level of meaning—that which incorporates the total significance of the words.

What does that mean? Beyond a literal definition, words communicate emotion, bias, attitude, and perspective. Analyzing any text involves learning to interpret what is implied, just as much as what is expressly stated.

15 Questions to Help You

Beyond grasping the meaning of words and phrases, critical reading requires that you ask questions. Here are 15 questions that will help you effectively analyze and interpret most of what you read:

1. Is a clear message communicated throughout?
2. Are the relationships between the points direct and clear?
3. Is there a relationship between your experience and the author's?
4. Are the details factual?
5. Are the examples and evidence relevant?
6. Is there consistency of thought?
7. What is the author's bias or slant?
8. What is the author's motive?
9. What does the author want you to believe?
10. Does this jibe with your beliefs or experiences?
11. Is the author rational or subjective?
12. Is there a confusion between feelings and facts?
13. Are the main points logically ordered?
14. Are the arguments and conclusions consistent?
15. Are the explanations clear?

Obviously, this list of questions is not all-inclusive, but it will give you a jump start when critical reading is required. Remember, the essential ingredient in any effective analysis and interpretation is the questions you ask.

Summarizing: The Final Step

Nothing will be more important to your recall than learning to condense what you read into a clear and concise summary.

Many of you have learned to do this by excerpting entire segments or sentences from a text—certainly not a very efficient method for summarizing. I recommend using the traditional outline.

Another suggestion is to use a two-step process called diagramming, which calls for the reader to diagram or illustrate the content he's just read, then write a brief synopsis of what he's learned.

Similar to outlining, diagramming helps the reader to visualize the relationships between various thoughts and ideas. Concept diagrams, or concept trees, are very useful visual aids for depicting the structure of a textbook.

Unless you have a photographic memory, you will find that recalling a picture of the main points will greatly increase what you remember. Beyond this, such diagrams require that you distill what is essential to the text and how it relates to the main message.

Suppose you read a chapter in your language arts class about the types of sciences. Your diagram might reduce your reading material to look like the following:

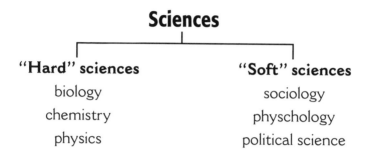

More than just a listing of main points, a diagram allows you to picture how parts fit together, which enhances your ability to recall the information you've read. This is especially true the more "visual" you are.

Distill It Into a Synopsis

The second step in the process of summarizing is to write a brief synopsis of what you've learned. When you need to review the material, diagrams will remind you of the significant elements in the text. Your synopsis will remind you of the main idea.

The goal here is to put in your own words what you gleaned from what you have read. You will find this process an invaluable gauge of whether you have understood the message—and on what level.

Use this method one chapter at a time, and do not proceed to the next chapter until you have completed the following exercise:

1. Write definitions of any key terms you feel are essential to understanding the topic.

2. Write questions and answers you feel clarify the topic.

3. Write any questions for which you don't have answers—then make sure you find them through rereading, further research, or asking another student or your teacher.

4. Even if you still have unanswered questions, move on to the next section and complete numbers 1 to 3 for that section. (And so on, until your reading assignment is complete.) See if this method doesn't help you get a better handle on any assignment right from the start.

Critical reading is not easy. It requires a lot more concentration and effort than the quick reference reading that you can get away with for much of your day-to-day class assignments. And I won't kid you—much of the reading you'll do in the latter years of high school and throughout college will be critical reading.

But if you follow the steps I've outlined for each critical reading assignment that you tackle—preparing yourself for the read, doing a preread skim followed by an analytical reading, concluding with a summarization—you'll discover that critical reading can be a much smoother, even rewarding, experience!

The Method You Probably Learned

If you were taught a specific reading method in school, it was probably the one developed back in the 1940s that is abbreviated "SQ3R." This stands for Survey, Question, Read, Recite, and Review. Here's how the process works.

Survey. Preread the chapter, concentrating on topic sentences, subheads, and review questions in order to get an overview of what's ahead.

Question. Once you've surveyed the chapter, ask yourself what information is contained in it. Consider turning the subheads into questions as an exercise.

Read. Now read the first section thoroughly, attempting to answer the questions you've posed. Take notes, highlight, underline, map.

Recite. Now answer the questions without looking at your notes or the text. When you're done, go on to the next section. Continue this detailed reading/ reciting tandem until you finish the chapter (or the assignment).

Review. Go back over the entire assignment.

Does this sound familiar? I agree. I think this method is completely incorporated into the steps I've outlined in this and previous chapters. Frankly, I think the detailed method I've proposed—and the helpful advice along the way—covers far more ground.

CHAPTER 7

READING THE LITERATURE

"Will you walk a little faster?" said a whiting to a snail. "There's a porpoise close behind us and he's treading on my tail!"

"If I'd been the whiting," said Alice, whose thoughts were still running on the song, "I'd have said to the porpoise, 'Keep back, please; we don't want you with us!'"

"They were obliged to have him with them," the Mock Turtle said. "No wise fish would go anywhere without a porpoise."

"Wouldn't it really?" said Alice in a tone of great surprise.

"Of course not," said the Mock Turtle. "Why, if a fish came to me, and told me he was going on a journey, I should say, 'With what porpoise?'"

"Don't you mean 'purpose'?" said Alice.

"I mean what I say," the Mock Turtle replied in an offended tone.

—Lewis Carroll, *Alice in Wonderland*

In this excerpt, you could enjoy the nonsensical picture of a porpoise pushing a snail and whiting to walk faster. You might laugh at the confusion of "porpoise" and "purpose" by the Mock Turtle. Or you could discern the message—that you need to have a purpose when you are on a journey… or reading.

Why should you care about literature? Who needs to read the book when you can see the movie?

While I didn't write this book to give you a lecture on the merits of the classics, please bear with me for a couple of paragraphs.

The Greatest Involvement Device

Unlike anything else, literature involves the reader in the story. How? There are no joysticks to manipulate, no "surround sound" to engulf you. Your imagination is your only involvement device, but it far surpasses any high-tech computer gimmick.

Your imagination makes reading the ultimate adventure. It allows you to immerse yourself in the story—identifying with the protagonist, fighting his battles, experiencing his fears, sharing his victories. You may become so involved, you end up staying up well past your bedtime, turning page after page late into the night!

Your imagination is the vehicle that allows you to explore a million different lives, from floating down the Mississippi River on a raft, to suffering through a star-crossed love affair, to having tea with the March Hare and Mad Hatter, as our Alice did.

Creative writing may be serious or humorous or sublime… or all three. It is often subtle; meanings are elusive and delicate. Such writing, when done effectively, evokes emotional responses. You get angry. You shed a tear. You chuckle. An author's expression strikes a chord that moves you. You and the author communicate on a level that is far beyond an exchange of facts and information.

Assuming that I have converted all you literature skeptics to avid library loiterers (and even if I haven't), I'll offer some advice to help you begin your journey to literary appreciation. It begins with understanding the basic road map.

Which Reading Method? Pleasure or Critical?

While I certainly encourage you to approach your reading with the enthusiasm and anticipation that would justify the pleasure-reading method (see Chapter 2), the demands of the teacher who assigns the reading will probably require the critical reading method.

Reading literature requires most of the skills we've discussed previously. There are devices and clues to ferret out that will help you follow the story and understand its meaning better. You will analyze and interpret what the author is saying and evaluate its worth.

But in addition, in literature you will be able to appreciate the words themselves. In textbooks, you often must penetrate a thick jungle of tangled sentences and murky paragraphs to find the information you seek.

Great literature is its language. It's the flow and ebb of its words, the cadence of its sentences, as much as it is story and theme.

As you read more, you'll uncover the diversity of tapestries that different authors weave with words. You may discover similar themes coursing through the works of authors like Ernest Hemingway or Thomas Hardy, but their use of language is as different as desert and forest. The composition of the words themselves is an element you'll want to examine as you read literature critically.

Fiction: Just Another Word for Storytelling

Most fiction is an attempt to tell a story. There is a beginning, in which the characters and the setting are introduced. There is a conflict or struggle (middle) that advances the story to a climax (end), where the conflict is resolved. A final denouement or "winding up" clarifies the conclusion of the story.

Your literature class will address all of these parts using literary terms that are often more confusing than helpful. The following are brief definitions of some of the more important ones.

Plot: The order or sequence of the story—how it proceeds from the opening through the climax. Your ability to understand and appreciate literature depends upon how well you follow the plot—the story.

Characterization: The personalities or characters central to the story—the heroes, heroines, and villains. You will want to identify the main characters of the story and their relationships to the struggle or conflict.

Theme: The controlling message or subject of the story; the moral or idea that the author is using the plot and characters to communicate. Some examples: man's inhumanity to man; man's impotency in his environment; the corrupting influence of power, greed, and unrequited love. Just as with nonfiction, you need to discern this theme to really understand what it is the author wants to communicate.

Setting: The time and place in which the story takes place. This is especially important when reading a historical novel or one that takes you to another culture.

Point of view: Who is telling the story? Is it one of the central characters giving you flashbacks or a first-person perspective? Or is it a third-person narrator offering commentary and observations on the characters, the setting, and the plot? This person moves the story along and gives it an overall tone.

The first step in reading literature is to familiarize yourself with these concepts, and then try to recognize them in each novel or short story you read.

The second step is the same as for reading nonfiction—to identify your purpose for reading.

Allow your purpose to define how you will read. If you are reading to be entertained, then a pleasure read is the way to go. If you're reading for a class and will be required to participate in discussions or be tested on the material, you'll want to do a critical read.

How Long Should It Take?

As a general rule, fiction is not meant to be read over a period of months—or even weeks. Try to read an assigned book or story as quickly as possible, fast enough to progress through the plot, get a sense of the characters and their struggles, and hear the author's message or theme.

It's helpful to set a goal as to when you want to finish your reading. Frequently, of course, this will already be set for you, if your reading is a class assignment.

You should, however, set daily goals. Set aside one or two hours to read, or set a goal of reading three chapters a day until you finish. Reading sporadically—10 minutes one day, a half hour the next, then not picking up the book until several days later—means that you'll lose track of the plot and characters and just as quickly lose interest.

Too often, when students do not establish a regular schedule, their reading becomes fragmented, making it very difficult to piece together the whole story. A reasonable goal is to try to read a novel in less than a week, a short story in one sitting.

If you try to read fiction more rapidly, you will greatly increase your enjoyment of it. It is vitally important that as you try to read faster, you give the story your full attention. By doing this you will be surprised by how improved your understanding and appreciation are.

To speed your reading of fiction, try this experiment:

1. Find a novel or short story that interests you and is relatively easy to read. Tomes like *Ulysses* or *The Naked Lunch* shouldn't be candidates.

2. Set aside two or three hours to invest in reading the book. If at all possible, finish it in one sitting. If you can't, then allocate the same amount of time each day until you do.

By trying this experiment, you will discover that fiction is intended to be read this way—in one sitting, whenever possible. It is as if you are sitting at a master storyteller's feet as he spins his tale. You want to know how the story ends and what happens to the hero.

Will the villain get his comeuppance? Will the hero get the girl? Or will he ride off with his horse?

You'll find that you appreciate the story far more at the end than anywhere in the middle.

Some other tips for reading fiction:

1. Understand the plot and maintain awareness of its progression.

2. Take breaks to review what has occurred and who is involved.

3. Vary your reading method, from skimming transitional bridge material to carefully reading descriptions and narration.

4. Question the story's theme. What is the message?

You're Allowed to Enjoy It

A final recommendation: Give yourself permission to enjoy what you are reading. You will be amazed at the difference this will make. Fiction, unlike any other reading, can take you on an adventure. Through your mind, you can journey to faraway lands, pretend you are someone else, feel emotions you may never otherwise experience. All this happens as you gain an appreciation of literature—as you learn to understand fiction and allow yourself to enjoy great stories.

CHAPTER 8

FOCUSING YOUR MIND

U nlike other activities, reading requires an active mind and a passive body. A deadly combination, especially when you've spent the day in classes and haven't had a chance to burn off that excess energy with a tennis match, a game of "hoops," or a quick run around campus.

Concentration-wise, reading can be more demanding than class lectures, homework assignments, or taking notes. In class, you at least have vocal variety and the threat of being called on to keep you focused. And writing, while a sedentary activity, still requires some hand-eye coordination to keep your brain working.

Keep Your Mind on One Thing

Concentration begins with the ability to keep your mind focused on one thing—your reading assignment. This is not an innate talent, but a learned discipline. Much like an athlete must learn to be so focused that she is completely unaffected by screaming crowds, a good reader absorbs himself in what he's reading.

How does your mind discipline "rate"? Answer these questions to find out:

1. When I read, do I often allow random thoughts to steal my focus?

2. As I read, am I easily distracted by noises or other activities?

3. Am I watching the clock to see how long I have to keep reading?

There is no simple, magic formula for conjuring up concentration—especially when you're faced with a critical reading assignment you're not particularly enamoured of. But if you follow the preparatory steps I've discussed in previous chapters—define your purpose, skim for a pre-read, identify questions for which you will seek answers—you should find it a bit easier to stay focused.

Steps to Better Concentration

Here are some other practical steps I recommend to increase your ability to concentrate:

1. **Get some exercise** before you begin your reading. A game of racquetball, an exercise class, a workout at the gym, even a brisk walk, will help burn off physical energy so you'll be able to direct all of your mental energy to your reading.

2. **Read in the right place.** No, it's not in front of the TV, nor in your room if your roommate is hosting a pizza party. Reading is a solitary activity. Find a quiet corner, preferably in a place designated for study only—at your desk or in the library. Although tempting, reading on your bed can be dangerous if you're struggling to concentrate. You just may lose the battle and find yourself in the perfect place to doze off.

3. **Eliminate distractions.** If you've properly scheduled your reading time, you won't be distracted by other pending assignments. If you're trying to read one assignment while worrying about another, your concentration—and comprehension—will inevitably suffer.

   Make sure there's nothing else in sight to vie for your attention. Are there letters on your desk that you need to answer? Put them away and schedule some time to write back. Do you hear sirens and screams from the TV show in the other room? Turn it off or down or, better yet, close your door.

4. **Plan breaks.** If you have three hours or more of reading ahead of you, the mere thought of it may be so discouraging that you'll lose your concentration before you even pick up the book. Schedule short 10- or 15-minute breaks after each hour of reading. Get up. Listen to some music. Stretch. If you must break more frequently, keep your breaks shorter. By dividing your reading into smaller, more digestible bites, you'll be able to concentrate more effectively.

Wait! Don't Start Reading Yet

Have you defined your purpose for reading? Once again, you must have a clearly defined purpose or goal. What are you reading for? (I have addressed this numerous times, but spaced repetition is a very effective way to make a point.) The point is that reading without purpose is the greatest means to getting nowhere, which is where you'll find your mind after about a half-hour.

Know why you are reading. If your teacher or professor has given you questions to answer, then you know what you're looking for. If not, ask your own questions, using the clues in your book (as discussed in Chapter 2).

An effective preread of the material should help you define your purpose and stimulate some interest in finding out more—which will result in increased concentration.

Motivation: Crucial to Concentration

Motivation is key to your success in just about any endeavor, whether it's graduating with honors, maintaining an effective time-management program, or improving your reading. You can utilize all the tricks and steps I've mentioned in this chapter, but if you lack the motivation to read, you'll still find it a struggle to concentrate on your assignments.

There are two types of motivation—intrinsic and extrinsic. What's the difference?

An avid murder mystery fan, you buy stacks of paperbacks at the used bookstore and spend your free time with your nose buried in them. You love the challenge of figuring out who's guilty before you reach the end. In fact, you'd spend all weekend reading mysteries if you didn't have to complete a reading assignment for your political science class. You're not particularly interested in that course, but your efforts on this assignment could secure you an A for the term, so you're determined to read the material and "ace" the exam.

Your motivation for reading the mysteries is intrinsic—you do it because you enjoy it. You don't get any awards. You don't get paid for it.

The poly sci reading, on the other hand, requires external motivation. You're reading it because you want to earn a high grade in class. Your reward is external—beyond the reading itself.

Whether you are intrinsically motivated to read or doing it for some external reward doesn't matter, as long as you are motivated by something! If you find it difficult to get excited about reading your economics assignment, remind yourself of how this exercise will help your grade. Get yourself externally motivated.

If that doesn't get you motivated enough to read for three hours, there's nothing wrong with a little bribery. Reward yourself with something more immediate. Promise yourself that if you stay focused on your reading until it's completed, you can rent the movie you've been wanting to see, or you can buy that new CD. (If you need lots of extrinsic motivation, you could run out of money!)

The value of concentration can be summed up in one statement: Concentration is essential to comprehension. Where there is failure to focus, there will be little or no understanding.

Without concentration, you will see only words on a page.

CHAPTER 9

RETAINING THE INFORMATION

The ultimate test of your comprehension is what you remember after you have finished your reading.

As a student, most of your reading will be for classes in which, sooner or later, you'll be required to regurgitate the information you've read in some type of format—essay test, term paper, multiple-choice, true/false, or fill-in-the-blank final.

So, beyond just being able to complete your reading assignments, you want to be sure you remember what you've read.

All of you have probably had the experience of forgetting that one fact that made the difference between an A- and a B+ (or a B- and a C+). It was sitting right there, on the tip of your brain, but you couldn't quite remember it.

Memory Can Be Improved

You probably know people with photographic (or near-photographic) memories. They know all the words to every song recorded in the last four years, remind you of things you said to them three years ago, and never forget anyone's birthday (or anniversary or "day we met" or "first kiss day," ad infinitum).

While some people seem to be able to retain information naturally, a good memory—like good concentration—can be learned. You can control what stays in your mind and what is forgotten.

Some people remember with relative ease and have no problem retaining large volumes of information. Others often are aggravated by a faulty memory that seems to lose more than it retains. Several factors contribute to your capability to recall information you take in.

- **Intelligence, age, and experience** all play a role in how well you remember. Not everyone remembers the same way. You need to identify how these factors affect your memory and learn to maximize your strengths.

- **Laying a strong foundation** is important to good memory. Most learning is an addition to something you already know. If you never grasped basic chemistry, then mastering organic chemistry will be virtually impossible. By developing a broad foundation of basic knowledge, you will enhance your ability to recall new information.

- **Motivation is key** to improving your memory. A friend of mine, the consummate baseball fan, seems to know every baseball statistic from the beginning of time. He can spout off batting averages and ERAs from any decade for virtually any player, his favorite team's season schedule...and most of the other teams', too! While I wouldn't say he is the most intelligent guy I've ever met, he obviously loves baseball and is highly motivated to learn everything he can about his favorite subject. You probably have a pet interest, too. Whether it's movies, music, or sports, you've filled your brain with a mountain of information. Now, if you can learn that much about one subject, you are obviously capable of retaining information about other subjects—even chemistry. You just have to learn how to motivate yourself.

- **A method, system, or process** for retaining information is crucial to increasing your recall. This may include organizing your thinking, good study habits, or mnemonic devices—some means that you utilize when you have to remember.

- **Using what you learn** right after you learn it is important to recall. It's fine to memorize a vocabulary list for a quick quiz, but if you wish to retain information for the long haul, you must reinforce your learning by using this knowledge. For example, you will add a new word to your permanent vocabulary if you make a point to use it, correctly, in a conversation.

The study of foreign languages, for many, proves frustrating when there are no opportunities outside of class to practice speaking the language. That's why foreign language students often join conversation groups or study abroad—to reinforce retaining what they've learned by using it.

Why We Forget

As you think about the elements of developing good memory, you can use them to address why you forget. The root of poor memory is usually found in one of these areas:

1. We fail to make the material meaningful.

2. We did not learn prerequisite material.

3. We fail to grasp what is to be remembered.

4. We do not have the desire to remember.

5. We allow apathy or boredom to dictate how we learn.

6. We have no set habit for learning.

7. We are disorganized and inefficient in our use of study time.

8. We do not use the knowledge we have gained.

All of us are inundated with information every day, bombarded with facts, concepts, and opinions. We are capable of absorbing some information simply because the media drench us with it. In order to retain most information, we have to make a concerted effort to do so. We must make this same effort with the material we read.

How to Remember

There are some basic tools that will help you remember what you read:

- **Understanding.** You will remember only what you understand. When you read something and grasp the message, you have begun the process of retention. The way to test this is to rephrase the message in your own words. Can you summarize the main idea? Unless you understand what is being said, you won't be able to decide whether to remember or discard it.

- **Desire.** Let me repeat: You remember what you choose to remember. If you do not want to retain some piece of information or don't believe you can, then you won't! To remember the material, you must want to remember it and be convinced that you will remember it.

- **Overlearn.** To ensure that you retain material, you need to go beyond simply doing the assignment. To really remember what you learn, you should learn material thoroughly, or overlearn. This involves prereading the text, doing a critical read, and having some definite means of review that reinforces what you should have learned.

- **Systematize.** It's more difficult to remember random thoughts or numbers than those organized in some pattern. For example, which phone number is easier to remember: 538–6284 or 678–1234? Once you recognize the pattern in the second number, it takes much less effort to remember than the first. You should develop the ability to discern the structure that exists and recall it when you try to remember. Have a system to help you recall how information is organized and connected.

- **Association.** It's helpful to attach or associate what you are trying to recall to something you already have in your memory. Mentally link new material to existing knowledge so that you are giving this new thought some context in your mind.

A Procedure to Improve Recall

Each time you attempt to read something that you must recall, use this six-step process:

1. **Evaluate the material and define your purpose** for reading. Identify your interest level and get a sense of how difficult the material is.

2. **Choose appropriate reading techniques** for the purpose of your reading.

3. **Identify the important facts.** Remember what you need to. Identify associations that connect the details you must recall.

4. **Take notes.** Use your own words to give a synopsis of the main ideas. Use an outline, diagram, or concept tree to show relationships and patterns. Your notes provide an important backup to your memory. Writing down key points will further reinforce your ability to remember.

5. **Review.** Quiz yourself on those things you must remember. Develop some system by which you review notes at least three times before you are required to recall. The first review should be shortly after you've read the material, the second a few days later, and the final just before you are expected to recall. This process will help you avoid cram sessions.

6. **Implement.** Find opportunities to use the knowledge you have gained. Study groups and class discussions are invaluable opportunities to implement what you've learned.

Memorizing and Mnemonics

There are some specific methods to help you recall when you must remember a lot of specific facts. The first of these is rote memorization—the process of trying to recall information word-for-word.

Memorize only when you are required to remember something for a relatively short time—when you have a history quiz on battle dates, a chemistry test on specific formulas, or a vocabulary test in French.

When memorization is required, you should do whatever is necessary to impress the exact information on your mind. Repetition is probably the most effective method. Write down the information on a 3 × 5 card and use it as a flashcard. You must quiz yourself frequently to assure that you know the information perfectly.

A second technique for recalling lots of details is mnemonics. A mnemonic device is used to help recall large bits of information which may or may not be logically connected. Such mnemonics are invaluable when you must remember facts not arranged in a clear fashion, items that are quite complicated, and numerous items that are a part of a series.

One of the simplest methods is to try to remember just the first letter of a sequence. That's how Roy G. Biv (the colors of the spectrum, in order from left to right—red, orange, yellow, green, blue, indigo, violet) came about. Or **E**very **G**ood **B**oy **D**oes **F**ine, to remember the notes on the musical staff. Or, perhaps the simplest of all, **FACE**, to remember the notes in between. (The latter two work opposite of old Roy—using words to remember letters.) Of course, not many sequences work out so nicely. If you tried to memorize the signs of the zodiac with this method, you'd wind up with **A**ries, **T**aurus, **G**emini, **C**ancer, **L**eo, **V**irgo, **L**ibra, **S**corpio, **S**agittarius, **C**apricorn, **A**quarius, **P**isces. Many of you may be able to make a name or a place or something out of ATGCLVLSSCAP, but I can't!

One solution is to make up a simple sentence that uses the first letters of the list you're trying to remember as the first letters of each word. To remember the zodiacal signs, just memorize the phrase **A T**all **G**iraffe **C**hewed **L**eaves **V**ery **L**ow; **S**ome **S**low **C**ows **A**t **P**lay.

Wait a minute! It's the same number of words. Why not just figure out some way to memorize the signs themselves? What's better about the second set? A couple of things. First of all, it's easier to picture the giraffe and cow and what they're doing. Creating mental images is a very powerful way to remember almost anything. Second, because the words in our sentence bear some relationship to each other, they're much easier to remember. Go ahead, try it. See how long it takes you to memorize the sentence as opposed to all the signs. This method is especially easy when you remember some or all of the items but don't remember their order.

Remember: Make your sentence(s) memorable to you. Any sentence or series of words that helps you remember these letters will do. Here are just two more I created in a few seconds: **A T**all **G**irl **C**alled **L**ovely **V**era **L**oved to **S**ip **S**odas from **C**ans **A**nd **P**lates. **A**ny **T**iny **G**erbil **C**ould **L**ove **V**enus. **L**ong **S**illy **S**nakes **C**ould **A**ll **P**ray. (Isn't it easy to make up memorably silly pictures in your head for these?)

You will find that in business or the classroom, mnemonic devices like this allow you to readily recall specific information that you need to retain for longer periods of time. They are especially useful if you have to remember chemical classifications, lines of music, and anatomical lists.

As effective as mnemonic devices are, don't try to create them for everything you have to remember. Why? To generate a device for everything you need to learn would demand more time than any one person has. And you just might have trouble remembering all the devices you created to help you remember in the first place! Too many mnemonics can make your retention more complicated and hinder effective recall.

Complex mnemonics are not very useful—they can be too difficult to memorize. When you choose to utilize a mnemonic, you should keep it simple so that it facilitates the quick recall you intended.

Many people complain that their mind is a sieve—everything they read slips through—and they never remember anything. I hope you now are convinced that this is a correctable problem. You don't have to be a genius to have good retention—you simply must be willing to work at gaining the skills that lead to proficient recall. As you master these skills, you will improve your reading by increasing your rate of retention.

CHAPTER 10

LET'S READ UP ON ADD

What is ADD (Attention Deficit Disorder)? It's probably easiest to describe as a person's difficulty with focusing on a single thing for any significant period of time. People with ADD are described as easily distracted, impatient, impulsive, and often seeking immediate gratification. They have poor listening skills and trouble doing "boring" jobs (like sitting quietly in class or, as adults, balancing a checkbook). "Disorganized" and "messy" are words that also come up often.

Hyperactivity, however, is more clearly defined as restlessness, resulting in excessive activity. Hyperactives are usually described as having "ants in their pants." ADHD is a combination of hyperactivity and ADD.

According to the American Psychiatric Association, a person has ADHD if he or she meets eight or more of the following paraphrased criteria:

1. Can't remain seated if required to do so.

2. Is easily distracted by extraneous stimuli.

3. Focusing on a single task is difficult.

4. Frequently begins another activity without completing the first.

5. Fidgets or squirms (or feels restless mentally).

6. Can't (or doesn't want to) wait for his turn during group activities.

7. Will often interrupt with an answer before a question is completed.

8. Has problems with chore or job follow-through.

9. Can't play quietly easily.

10. Impulsively jumps into physically dangerous activities without weighing the consequences.

11. Easily loses things (pencils, tools, papers) necessary to complete school or work projects.

12. Interrupts others inappropriately.

13. Talks impulsively or excessively.

14. Doesn't seem to listen when spoken to.

Three caveats to keep in mind: The behaviors must have started before age seven, not represent some other form of classifiable mental illness, and occur more frequently than in the average person of the same age.

Characteristics of People with ADD

Let's look at the characteristics generally ascribed to people with ADD in more detail:

Easily distracted. Since ADD people are constantly "scoping out" everything around them, focusing on a single item is difficult. Just try having a conversation with an ADD person while a television is on.

Short, but very intense, attention span. Though it can't be defined in terms of minutes or hours, anything ADD people find boring immediately loses their attention. Other projects may hold their rapt and extraordinarily intense attention for hours or days.

Disorganization. ADD children are often chronically disorganized—their rooms are messy, their desks are a shambles, their files incoherent. While people without ADD can be equally messy and disorganized, they can usually find what they are looking for; ADDers can't.

Distortions of time sense. ADDers have an exaggerated sense of urgency when they're working on something and an exaggerated sense of boredom when they have nothing interesting to do.

Difficulty following directions. A new theory on this aspect holds that ADDers have difficulty processing auditory or verbal information. A major aspect of this difficulty involves the very common reports of parents of ADD kids who say their kids love to watch TV and hate to read.

Daydreaming, falling into depressions, or having mood swings.

Take risks. ADDers seem to make faster decisions than non-ADDers.

Easily frustrated and impatient. ADDers do not beat around the bush or suffer fools gladly. They are direct and to the point. When things aren't working, "Do something!" is the ADD rallying cry, even if that something is a bad idea.

Why Do ADD Kids Have Trouble in School?

What should you look for in a school setting to make it more palatable to an ADDer? What can you do at home to help your child (or yourself)?

- **Learning needs to be project- and experience-based,** providing more opportunities for creativity and shorter and smaller "bites" of information. Many "gifted" programs offer exactly such opportunities. The problem for many kids with ADD is that they've spent years in nongifted classroom settings and may be labeled with underachieving behavior problems, effectively shut out of the programs virtually designed for them! Many parents report that children diagnosed as ADD, who failed miserably in public school, thrived in private school. What characterizes many private schools? Smaller classrooms and more individual attention with specific goal-setting, project-based learning. These factors are just what make ADD kids thrive!

- **Create a weekly performance template** on which both teacher and parent chart the child's performance, positive and negative.

- **Encourage special projects for extra credit.** Projects give ADDers the chance to learn in the mode that's most appropriate to them. They will also give such kids the chance to make up for the "boring" homework they sometimes simply can't make themselves do.

- **Stop labeling them as "disordered."** Kids react to labels, especially negative ones, even more than adults do.

▪ **Think twice about medication,** but don't discard it as an option. Many experts are concerned about the long-term side effects of the drugs normally prescribed for ADDers. On the other hand, if an ADD child cannot have his special needs met in a classroom, not medicating him may be a disaster.

Specific Suggestions About Reading

▪ **Practice, practice, practice.** ADDers will tend to have trouble reading, preferring visual stimulation to the "boring" words. Turn off the TV. Minimize time spent with PlayStation or other such games. ADDers may well be extraordinarily focused on such visual input and stimulating games, but only to the detriment of their schoolwork. Where possible, though, utilize videos, computers, interactive multimedia, and other forms of communication more attuned to ADDers to help them learn. There is a tremendous amount of educational software and CD-ROM material that may work better for ADDers than traditional printed books.

However, ADDers must obviously learn to read and practice reading. I would suggest finding a professional or a program to deal with your or your child's probable reading problems. Anything you can do to make reading more fun and interesting should be explored.

▪ **Break everything into specific goal units.** ADDers are very goal-oriented; as soon as they reach one, it's on to the next. Reestablishing very short-term, "bite-size" goals is essential. Make goals specific, definable, and measurable, and stick to only one priority at a time.

- **Create distraction-free zones.** Henry David Thoreau (who evidently suffered from ADD, by the way) was so desperate to escape distraction he moved to isolated Walden Pond. Organize your time and workspace to create your own "Walden Pond," especially when you have to read, write, take notes, or study. ADDers need silence, so consider the library. Another tip: Clean your work area thoroughly at the end of each day. This will minimize distractions as you try to read.

- **Train their attention span.** ADDers will probably never be able to train themselves to ignore distractions totally, but a variety of meditation techniques might help them stay focused longer.

- **Utilize short-term rewards.** ADD salespeople don't do well when a sales contest lasts for 6 months, even if the reward is, say, a 10-day cruise. But stick a $100 bill on the wall and watch them focus! Those with ADD are not motivated by rewards that are too ephemeral or too far in the future. They live for the here and now and need to be rewarded immediately.

I want to thank Thom Hartmann, author of *Attention Deficit Disorder: A Different Perception* (Underwood Books, 1997), from which I have freely and liberally borrowed (with his permission) for this chapter.

CHAPTER 11

BUILD YOUR OWN LIBRARY

"The reading of all good books is like
conversation with the finest men of past centuries."
—Descartes

I f you are ever to become an active, avid reader, access to books will do much to cultivate the habit. I suggest you "build" your own library. Your selections can and should reflect your own tastes and interests, but try to make them wide and varied. Include some of the classics, contemporary fiction, poetry, and biographies.

Save your high school and college texts—especially those from any English composition or writing classes. You'll be amazed at how some of the material retains its relevance. And try to read a good newspaper every day so as to keep current and informed.

Your local librarian can refer you to any number of lists of the "great books," most of which are available in inexpensive paperback editions. Here are four more lists—compiled by yours truly—of "great" classical authors; "great" not-so-classical authors, poets, and playwrights; some contemporary "pretty greats"; and a selection of my own favorite "great" books.

You may want to incorporate these on your to-buy list, especially if you're planning a summer reading program.

I'm sure that I have left off someone's favorite author or "important" title from these lists. So be it. They are not meant to be comprehensive, just relatively representative. I doubt anyone would disagree that a person familiar with the majority of authors and works listed would be considered well-read!

Who are Derek Walcott, Kenzaburo Oe, Nadine Gordimer, Octavio Paz, and Camilo Jose Cela? All winners of the Nobel Prize for Literature (1989 to 1994, along with Toni Morrison in 1993). I'm willing to bet a year's royalties not one of you reading this has heard of more than one of them (with the exception of Ms. Morrison). So how do you define "great" if these award winners are so anonymous? I include this merely to dissuade another 200 or so letters castigating me for some of those authors or works I did include in these lists.

Some "Great" Classical Authors

Aeschylus	Chaucer	Hegel	Pindar
Aesop	Cicero	Homer	Plato
Aquinas	Confucius	Horace	Plutarch
Aristophanes	Dante	S. Johnson	Rousseau
Aristotle	Descartes	Kant	Santayana
Balzac	Dewey	Machiavelli	Shakespeare
Boccaccio	Emerson	Milton	Spinoza
Burke	Erasmus	Montaigne	Swift
J. Caesar	Flaubert	Nietzsche	Vergil
Cervantes	Goethe	Ovid	Voltaire

Some Other "Great" Authors

Sherwood Anderson	T.S. Eliot
W.H. Auden	William Faulkner
Jane Austen	Edna Ferber
Samuel Beckett	F. Scott Fitzgerald
Brandan Behan	Ford Madox Ford
William Blake	E.M. Forster
Bertolt Brecht	Robert Frost
Charlotte Bronte	John Galsworthy
Emily Bronte	Jose Ortega y Gasset
Pearl Buck	Nikolai Gogol
Samuel Butler	Maxim Gorki
Lord Byron	Thomas Hardy
Albert Camus	Nathaniel Hawthorne
Lewis Carroll	Ernest Hemingway
Joseph Conrad	Hermann Hesse
e.e. cummings	Victor Hugo
Daniel Defoe	Aldous Huxley
Charles Dickens	Washington Irving
Emily Dickinson	Henry James
John Dos Passos	William James
Feodor Dostoevski	James Joyce
Arthur Conan Doyle	Franz Kafka
Theodore Dreiser	M.M. Kaye
Alexandre Dumas	John Keats
Lawrence Durrell	Rudyard Kipling
George Eliot	Arthur Koestler

D.H. Lawrence

Jack London

H.W. Longfellow

James Russell Lowell

Thomas Mann

W. Somerset Maugham

Herman Melville

H.L. Mencken

Henry Miller

H.H. Munro (Saki)

Vladimir Nabokov

O. Henry

Eugene O'Neill

George Orwell

Dorothy Parker

Edgar Allan Poe

Ezra Pound

Marcel Proust

Ellery Queen

Ayn Rand

Erich Maria Remarque

Bertrand Russell

J.D. Salinger

George Sand

Carl Sandburg

William Saroyan

Jean Paul Sartre

George Bernard Shaw

Percy Bysshe Shelley

Upton Sinclair

Aleksandr I. Solzhenitsyn

Gertrude Stein

Robert Louis Stevenson

Dylan Thomas

James Thurber

J.R.R. Tolkien

Leo Tolstoy

Ivan Turgenev

Mark Twain

Robert Penn Warren

Evelyn Waugh

H.G. Wells

Walt Whitman

Oscar Wilde

Thornton Wilder

Tennessee Williams

P.G. Wodehouse

Thomas Wolfe

Virginia Woolf

William Wordsworth

William Butler Yeats

Emile Zola

Some "Pretty Great" Contemporary Authors

Edward Albee

Isaac Asimov

James Baldwin

John Barth

Saul Bellow

T. Coraghessan Boyle

Anthony Burgess

Truman Capote

John Cheever

Don DeLillo

Pete Dexter

E.L. Doctorow

J.P. Donleavy

William Gaddis

William Golding

Dashiell Hammett

Robert Heinlein

Joseph Heller

Lillian Hellman

John Hersey

Oscar Hijuelos

Jerzy Kozinski

Malcolm Lowry

Norman Mailer

Bernard Malamud

Gabriel Garcia Marquez

Cormac McCarthy

Carson McCullers

Toni Morrison

Joyce Carol Oates

Flannery O'Connor

Thomas Pynchon

Philip Roth

Isaac Bashevis Singer

Jane Smiley

Wallace Stegner

Rex Stout

William Styron

Anne Tyler

John Updike

Alice Walker

Eudora Welty

Some "Great" Works

The Adventures of
    Huckleberry Finn

The Aeneid

Aesop's Fables

The Age of Innocence

The Alexandra Quartet

Alice In Wonderland

All the King's Men

All Quiet On the Western
    Front

An American Tragedy

Animal Farm

Anna Karenina

Arrowsmith

As I Lay Dying

Atlas Shrugged

Babbitt

The Bell Jar

Beloved

Beowulf

The Bonfire of the Vanities

Brave New World

The Brothers Karamazov

The Canterbury Tales

Catch-22

The Catcher in the Rye

A Clockwork Orange

Confessions of an English
    Opium Eater

The Confessions of Nat Turner

The Count of Monte Cristo

Crime and Punishment

David Copperfield

Death Comes for the
    Archbishop

Death of a Salesman

The Deerslayer

Demian

Don Juan

Don Quixote

Ethan Fromme

Far From the Madding Crowd

A Farewell to Arms

The Federalist Papers

The Fixer

For Whom the Bell Tolls

The Foundation

From Here to Eternity

The Ginger Man

The Good Earth

The Grapes of Wrath

Gravity's Rainbow

The Great Gatsby

Gulliver's Travels

Hamlet

Heart of Darkness

Henderson the Rain King

The Hound of the
   Baskervilles

I, Claudius

The Idiot

The Iliad

The Immortalist

The Invisible Man

Jane Eyre

JR

Julius Caesar

Kim

King Lear

Lady Chatterley's Lover

"Leaves of Grass"

The Legend of Sleepy
   Hollow

Les Miserables

A Long Day's Journey into
   Night

Look Homeward, Angel

Lord Jim

Lord of the Flies

The Lord of the Rings

Macbeth

The Magic Mountain

Main Street

Man and Superman

The Merchant of Venice

The Metamorphosis

Moby Dick

The Naked and the Dead

Native Son

1984

Of Human Bondage

Of Mice and Men

The Old Man and the Sea

Oliver Twist

One Flew over the Cuckoo's
   Nest

The Optimist's Daughter

Othello

Our Town

Paradise Lost

The Pickwick Papers

The Picture of Dorian Gray

A Portrait of the Artist as
   a Young Man

Portrait of a Lady

Pride and Prejudice

The Prophet

Ragtime

"The Raven"

The Red Badge of Courage

The Remembrance of
    Things Past

The Return of the Native

Robinson Crusoe

Romeo and Juliet

The Scarlet Letter

Siddhartha

Silas Marner

Sister Carrie

Slaughterhouse Five

Sons and Lovers

Sophie's Choice

The Sound and the Fury

Steppenwolf

A Streetcar Named Desire

The Sun Also Rises

The Tale of Genji

A Tale of Two Cities

Tender Is the Night

The Thin Red Line

The Time Machine

A Thousand Acres

Tom Jones

The Trial

Ulysses

U.S.A. (trilogy)

Vanity Fair

Walden

War and Peace

"The Wasteland"

The Way of All Flesh

Wuthering Heights

Reading every one of these books will undoubtedly make you a better reader; it will certainly make you more well-read. The added bonus to establishing such a reading program is an appreciation of certain authors, books, cultural events, and the like that separates the cultured from the merely educated and the undereducated.

Read on and enjoy.

CHAPTER 12

READING:
A LIFELONG ACTIVITY

"And further, by these, my son, be admonished:
making many books there is no end..."
—Solomon (Ecclesiastes 12:12)

Well, you made it through another book. I hope you found the motivation—whether intrinsic or extrinsic—to define your purpose, discern the important details, grasp the main idea, and retain what you read. I promised not to preach about the joys of reading. And I haven't...too much.

Your need to read—and comprehend and retain what you read—will not end when you graduate from school.

Planning on working? From the very first week, when you're given the employee handbook, you'll be expected to seek out the facts—like what happens if you're late more than twice.

You'll be required to read critically—and understand the meaning of statements like "Our dress code requires professional attire at all times."

Business proposals, annual reports, patient charts, corporate profiles, product reports, sales reports, budget proposals, business plans, resumes, complaint letters, interoffice memos—no matter what type of work you do, you won't be able to avoid the avalanche of paper and required reading that accompanies it.

Not only will your job require the ability to read and comprehend, but so will other facets of your life. If you plan to buy a house, wait until you see the pile of paperwork you'll have to wade through.

Credit card applications? Better read the fine print to make sure you know when your payment must be in…and how much interest you're paying on that brand-new TV.

Insurance policies, appliance warranties, local ordinances, newspapers, membership applications, and tax forms—it seems like any goal you pursue in your life will require you to scale mountains of reading material.

For your own best interest, you must be prepared to read—and understand.

I wish you the greatest possible success in your future reading pursuits, of which there will be many…throughout your life.

INDEX

About the Author

Ron Fry is a nationally known spokesperson for the improvement of public education and an advocate for parents and students playing an active role in strengthening personal education programs. In addition to being the author of the vastly popular *How to Study Program*, Fry has edited or written more than 30 different titles— resources for optimum student success.

"Helpful for students of all ages from high school and up."
– Small Press Book Review

"These are must-read guides every family should have in its library."
– Library Journal

How to Study Series:

- ■ **How to Study**
- ■ **"Ace" Any Test**
- ■ **Get Organized**
- ■ **Improve Your Memory**
- ■ **Improve Your Writing**
- ■ **Improve Your Reading**

For product information and technology assistance, contact us at

Cengage Learning Customer & Sales Support,
1-800-354-9706.

Endorsements for
Pursuing Life
with a Shepherd's Heart

"Leo Tolstoy, in a time of spiritual bewilderment, learned the purpose of life from a shepherd. In our interactions with animals, we can learn wonderful things about God's relationship with us. Ken Johnson found this out while raising sheep, and he has passed on some powerful principles of life that will be beneficial to the reader." – *Al Quie, author of* Riding the Divide *and former Governor of Minnesota*

"Ken Johnson has been both a shepherd of sheep and a shepherd of men in his life's experience. Hence he is expert at drawing parallels between the two and pointing both men and women to the Great Shepherd – our Lord and Savior Jesus Christ. All of us have 'sheep' in our lives – children, neighbors, friends and colleagues. It is up to us to recognize that God expects us to *be* shepherds to some particular group that He has placed under our area of influence. Ken's book does an excellent job of reminding us of this evangelical nurturing truth." – *Cary Humphries, Chair of Northwestern College in St. Paul, Minnesota, and retired Senior Vice President of Cargill, Inc.*

"Gideon was threshing wheat. Elisha was plowing his field. Ezra was serving the king. Peter was mending his nets. Ken Johnson is ministering in the business world. Each of these men was honored by a direct call from God." – *Bob Foster, founder of Lost Valley Ranch, Sedalia, Colorado*

"This book is timeless! Practical truths that Ken Johnson so engagingly describes in *Pursing Life With a Shepherd's Heart* are needed now more than ever." – *William E. Brown, President, Cedarville University*

Pursuing Life

with a
Shepherd's Heart

Practical Perspectives From the Flock
For Everyday Realities at Home and at Work

By Ken Johnson
with Robert J. Tamasy

Pursuing Life
with a Shepherd's Heart

Scripture References from the New American
Standard Bible, (NASB), Copyright: 1960, 1962,
1963, 1968, 1971, 1972, 1973, 1975, 1977 and
1995; by the Lockman Foundation.
Used with permission.

ISBN No. 0-9764232-0-0

Cover Design:
Dianne & Chris Holland Tuve
Minneapolis, MN
Graphic Layout:
Sara Jo Johnson
Roseville, MN
Editor:
Robert J. Tamasy
Hixson, TN
Published by:
River City Press
4301 Emerson Avenue N.
Minneapolis, MN 55412
1-888-234-3559

Dedication

To my beautiful wife, Ardie, whose life has served as a pattern for all the lessons this book offers, from her early childhood to the present.

She was a shepherdess in her youth, and her experiences woven into our family have been — and continue to be — priceless. A dear partner and a loving wife and mother: To her this book is dedicated, with our prayers that many will benefit from its content.

Ken Johnson

TABLE OF CONTENTS

Introduction

If you're like most people, your personal knowledge and understanding of sheep is extremely limited. What you know about them probably consists of some wool sweaters or slacks, maybe the lamb chop you ate for dinner one evening, or the old nursery rhyme, "Mary Had A Little Lamb." Unless you live in New Zealand, where the sheep population outnumbers the people, those wooly creatures probably don't contribute to the fabric of your neighborhood.

I used to be the same way, until some years ago when – at the urging of my wife, Ardie, who had grown up on a farm – we bought a 24-acre tract outside of St. Paul, Minnesota that became our "hobby farm." As I will explain later, we did not choose to raise sheep to fulfill a lifelong dream; we did it quite honestly because we had determined they were the easiest and most efficient way of maintaining our property. Fourteen years later, when we sold the last of my sheep to the local stockyard company, my family and I had become wealthy, not with money but with rich experiences and insights into the life and behavior of sheep. In the process, we had also gained a deeper understanding about people – and the ways we think and act, personally and professionally.

Recent years have given us a variety of books that draw analogies from the animal world – sharks, mice, eagles, cats and dogs are just a few that come to mind. But there are relatively few books that regard sheep as a legitimate source for gaining insights into successful living, whether it's at work, in the home, in our churches or in our communities. This is not surprising. Sheep are notoriously unintelligent, misguided and basically, helpless. Given this reality, I have observed that sheep and people have striking, even unsettling, similarities in a number of areas, and I think that each of us – as husbands and wives, parents, employers and employees, friends and volunteers – would do ourselves a good service by paying heed to the bleat of a sheep.

There is one book in particular that does make ample use of sheep as case studies for how to live and work – and how not to. It's the Bible: It tells the story of a lowly shepherd boy who became king but never forgot what his sheep had taught him; it features a prophet who warned his people of the dangers of acting like sheep; and it presents stories about how shepherds should respond when sheep become lost or encounter trouble.

Most of us who have spent any time reading the Bible at all probably have considered passages such as, "All of us *like sheep* have gone astray, each of us has turned to his own way..." (Isaiah 53:6), with some detachment. After all, if we have not spent a lot of time around sheep, it's hard to say, "Hey, I can relate to that!" But after years of feeding, protecting and caring for ewes and rams – even participating in the birth of one balky little lamb – I can attest to why the Scriptures choose to compare people more frequently to sheep than to owls, horses, lions or foxes.

A friend once commented about a church he usually passed each morning while driving to work. It was called the Church of the Good Shepherd. The friend, a successful businessman, commented, "If I were a member of that church, it would mean, then, that I am a sheep. I really don't like that association. Sheep are pretty dumb animals, aren't they?"

Definitely an astute observation. However, I have come to the conclusion that divinely inspired parallels between sheep and people are not intended as an insult. In fact, from the beginning of the Bible, God declares that humankind is His foremost and favorite creation. We are "created in His own image," as Genesis 1:27 tells us, yet He ironically persists in linking us to those funny creatures who wear their woolen linings on the outside. In fact, the word *sheep* appears more than 120 times in the Scriptures. Adding words like *shepherd, lambs, flock* and *fold* raises the total well into the hundreds.

I don't write as the foremost authority on sheep and their idiosyncrasies. I'm a businessman by profession and have spent most of my working career in managing people and consulting with executives and business leaders. However, over the years I have discovered that whenever I have shared some of my sheep observations while speaking at a conference or seminar, in churches or private conversations, the response of many of my listeners has been fascination. For some of them, the revelation of the similarities we share with sheep has become one of life's delightful "aha!" moments.

When the last of my sheep and I parted ways in 1982, my sideline as a part-time shepherd came to an end. (Although anyone who has worked with sheep at all knows, "part-time" is a misnomer, since sheep have ways of gaining more of your attention than you ever intended to give.) My custom had been to rise early, tend to the needs of my little flock and then head to my office at the Northwestern Bell Telephone Company. When I returned home, the sheep usually were my first priority as well. I came to regard myself as a sort of shepherd in a three-piece suit.

While the lessons my sheep taught me had particular relevance for my working career, I found they also applied to people in every walk of life – custodians and corporate executives, airline pilots and athletes, heart specialists and homemakers, politicians and police officers. It's my pleasure to share some of these insights with you; if they make you feel a bit "sheepish," I will consider that I have accomplished my mission.

Just to whet your appetite, let me tell you something that I learned about the aforementioned Bo Peep: She was wrong! If you leave a lamb alone, it's highly unlikely that it will come home wagging its tail behind it. Sheep cannot be left alone to fend for themselves, at least not for long. If they don't receive consistent care and attention, they will find all manner of difficulties to get themselves into – including some situations that literally could become matters of life and death.

We can readily see how this truth about sheep relates to the "sheep" we live and work with every day. It's essential to remain in tune with members of our family, seeking to recognize their needs, as well as understand what they are thinking and feeling. It's also important to stay in touch with employees and what they require – and not just by occasional, impersonal e-mails, notes or voicemail. Whether it's the newest or oldest member of our family, the most recent addition to our staff or the senior-most member of the team, we all need attention and even good, old-fashioned TLC from time to time. If we leave people alone, they might not come home either – they might just wander off and find themselves in all sorts of difficulty or distress.

As you continue on, please indulge me in my suspicion that God may well have created sheep primarily to serve as object lessons to teach us more about ourselves. The useful properties of wool, as well as the tastiness of lamb chops, may have been included as a bonus to give us reason to keep sheep close enough to observe their all-too-human quirks.

As I share some of my sheep-raising experiences, decide for yourself: Are we really *like* sheep? Strange as it may seem, getting a little better acquainted with these simple but lovable animals could serve to equip us to perform better in the business world, not only for fulfilling our own purposes but also for meeting the needs of our family members, friends, and fellow workers. Ultimately, I hope it will give you a clearer picture of how you can live for and serve the Lord more effectively. After all,

"It is He who has made us, and not we ourselves; we are His people and the sheep of His pasture" (Psalm 100:3).

– Ken Johnson
Stillwater, MN 2004

Chapter One:
A SPECIAL DELIVERY
LESSON IN TEAMWORK

"He said to them, 'Tend My lambs....' " – John 21:15

Settling into the driver's seat of my car and closing the door, I felt the tension of the day begin to subside. It had been a hectic nine hours of non-stop meetings, problem-solving and decision-making. Just a normal day at the office. I thought about how much we take for granted the act of making a simple telephone call. When we pick up the phone to make a call, we rightfully expect the instrument and transmission lines to function properly so the call can be completed almost instantaneously. It was my job at Northwestern Bell—and that of the people who reported to me—to make sure those expectations were met. It's amazing how quickly the inability to make an important phone call can incite the wrath of an otherwise calm, sane human being.

On this particular day I felt I had more than earned my pay after dealing with an endless procession of problems. I looked forward to getting home and being able to retreat from my working realm that today, more than 30 years later, has grown into what is now

1

broadly termed as "telecommunications." The thirty-minute drive from St. Paul to rural Lake Elmo itself was therapeutic, providing me with time to unwind, put events of the day behind me, and mentally change hats from manager to family man.

It was early spring and I enjoyed the final moments of the day, even though it was gray and overcast, since I had spent most of the day indoors with nothing more appealing to look at than plain office walls. Warmth had not yet made its seasonal return to the frozen frontier we fondly know as Minnesota. Winter's brisk bite continued to hold fast, as did the layer of frosty white that had coated the countryside for months. Appearances notwithstanding, my calendar reassured me that the land would soon be undergoing a rebirth. Without visible evidence, native Minnesotans have learned to accept this on faith, clinging annually to our hope of release from icy bondage.

Lake Elmo was a community my family and I had grown to love. It was close enough to the city for convenience and a reasonable commute to work, yet far enough for us to escape the hubbub of urban living. It also provided us with opportunities that city life could not afford, including such diversions as raising sheep. For me, this basically amounted to the best of both worlds—work in the city and private life in the country.

While still a few miles from home, I reminded myself that this would not be a normal evening in the Johnson household. (This observation, in retrospect, may have been one of the greatest understatements of my life.) My wife, Ardie, was 100 miles away, visiting with her mother in the Minnesota town of Sandstone.

That was not unusual; after our children became old enough to care for themselves for an hour or two until I got home, she occasionally would make the brief trip north. Of course, at such times this meant that I would have to wear the dual hats of dad and mom.

I began running down my mental checklist: What should we have for supper? Will the kids need me to help them with their homework? Tonight's Wednesday, right? That means we will have to be ready for church by 7:15.

Our little flock of sheep also came to my mind, and I knew they would need my attention ASAP. Although we were not vocational farmers, this pleasant "pastime" required a lot more work and commitment than most hobbies. Topping it off, spring is lambing season and our ewes were due to deliver very soon. "I wonder how they're doing?" I asked myself. Almost before I knew it, this question would force other, more mundane concerns such as supper and homework into the background.

We lived on a 24-acre farm, and our house sat about 150 feet off the road, hidden behind the trees from anyone who passed by. For this reason our large, weather-beaten mailbox that stood proudly at the front of the driveway seemed like a "Welcome Home" sign to me. It was always a friendly sight, especially after demanding workdays such as I had just endured— even at those times when I felt tempted to attach a trash receptacle to the back of it to collect junk mail, advertising circulars and bills.

On this particular evening, the mailbox was not standing alone. My eight-year-old son, Jim, was waiting for me, too. Even though Jim and I enjoyed a close relationship, he was never that eager to greet me, so my immediate—and accurate—thought was, "Something's up." I had a strong suspicion that my plans for the night were about to be reshuffled in a major way.

In the few moments remaining before I reached the driveway and an obviously agitated son, I reviewed the possibilities: Was there a problem at school? Maybe Jim's report card wasn't very good and he was hoping somehow to head off the consequences? Could the furnace have gone out? (On March days in Minnesota, thermal underwear is still in fashion.) Perhaps there was an urgent message from Ardie? Or could Jimmy be waiting with a news bulletin from the sheep nursery?

Anxiousness was etched in Jim's face. Usually, on a scale of one to ten, his range of expressed emotion would hover around two or three, but as I braked the car and rolled down the window, I saw he was about to jump out of his snow boots with excitement.

Frantically, he tried blurting out his assessment of the situation facing us. Some people are skilled at writing in shorthand; Jim was trying to communicate with me in "short-speak." His words came pouring out too fast for me to comprehend, so I finally held up my hand, asked him to stop and take a breath, and then start over. "Tell me again, slower. What's our problem?"

"There's a head sticking out of one of the ewes!" he exclaimed.

This simple, graphic description quickly eliminated the other possible scenarios I had been considering. However, since this is the normal way for a lamb to be born, I knew there had to be more to merit Jim's concern. He hastily explained the lamb had been in that position for some time, and its mother seemed to be having great difficulty with the delivery. Although I lacked a B.S. (bachelor of shepherding) and in my few years of raising sheep had observed only a small number of lambs being born, I knew what my son had described did not sound right. Usually, once a lamb pokes its head out of the womb, birth is just seconds away.

I told Jim to jump into the car and we drove to the house, parking in front and immediately trudging through the snow to the barn, which was about 100 yards away. I knew the struggling ewe would not notice—or care—whether her shepherd was wearing a business suit or overalls. As we neared the barn, I could tell my son's appraisal was correct. I heard low moaning coming from the ewe, indicating that she was in considerable distress. Walking through the door, I saw the mother sheep lying on her side, helpless. Judging from the straw, dirt and other matter stuck to her wooly coat, I could tell that she had been writhing in agony on the floor. The lamb's tiny, moist head that protruded from the mom's womb was also covered with debris, its eyes closed. It was not an appealing scene. Although I didn't know for certain, my initial thought was, "There is one dead lamb."

Rapidly trying to analyze the situation, I didn't have to overcome great waves of optimism. I knew something needed to be done, but was not sure what that was. Jim and I hurried back to the house so I could change into clothes more suited for whatever I would determine was necessary. I had been dressed for success in the business world, but a suit and tie were definitely out of style for a lamb birthing.

To be honest, I had doubts about how much help we could provide for the unfortunate ewe and her new offspring. I did realize that if this delivery were to be a success, it would require more than my urban-oriented ingenuity. For a veteran sheepherder, this might not have been a big deal, just another day "at the office." But for me, it presented a major crisis. In my years of experience in management with the telephone company, I hadn't received any training to prepare me for this. For the moment, however, my "avocation" was proving even more stressful than the workday I had just completed.

I have long advocated the motto, "When in doubt, pray," so I did—out loud. "Lord, we're really going to need your help with this one. I know that is one of your creatures out there in the barn struggling to get into this world, so I would appreciate your wisdom for what we should do."

While changing clothes, I evaluated my options. If Ardie had been home, I could have counted on her advice and on-site assistance. As a girl, she had grown up on a farm and had helped in raising her family's sheep. Her training as a registered nurse also would have come in handy. Jim apparently was thinking along the same lines when he suggested, "Let's call Mom!" I pointed out that she was too far away to be of any practical assistance—we were on our own in this one.

Our next-door neighbor was the next option. He was the local authority on sheep, having raised them for quite a few years. In fact, it was at his urging that we had gotten started with the animals, so I dialed his phone number. There is a shortcoming of telephones that even Northwestern Bell was never able to solve: If the person you want to talk with is not home, the phone won't do much immediate good. (Remember, this was years before anyone ever envisioned the widespread use of cell phones, or even call-forwarding and answering machines.) So when my neighbor failed to pick up his phone, I knew that we had come down to our final option.

"Well, Jim," I conceded, "We've got to try and see what we can do to help the ewe." We summoned my 12-year-old daughter, Janelle, from her room and advised her that we would need her assistance. She had just settled down to do her homework, and I could tell by her less-than-enthusiastic response that she was not excited about venturing back into the cold to help some "dumb old sheep." But with my firm, fatherly persuasion, she bundled up and joined us as we retraced our tracks through the snow to the barn.

When we arrived, it was evident that the ewe's dilemma had not improved. She appeared even more exhausted from the additional time and energy that had been expended. Squatting down to inspect more closely, I discovered the problem. Normally, a lamb is born with its front feet and forelegs coming out at the same time as the head. In this case, however, the forelegs had remained behind the head and a shoulder was preventing the lamb from sliding down the ewe's birth canal as it was supposed to do. After all this time, it was clear that the lamb was not going to work itself out, so the only course of action was for me to try pulling it out.

This may sound simple, but it wasn't. For one thing,

I have very large hands. It would not be an easy task to slip my hand into that small opening—particularly with a lamb already blocking the way. But there was no other recourse. Just as I had observed in business that there are times when it's necessary to do the unorthodox or unprecedented to solve a problem, it was the same in this case. Big mitts or not, I resolved to try working my hand inside the ewe and somehow maneuver the lamb's shoulder around so I could pull it out unimpeded.

Janelle's role in this process was to hold the ewe steady and keep her calm. In her weakened condition, the sheep offered no resistance to my daughter's firm grasp. Meanwhile, Jim had decided to do the best thing he could think of: He retreated to a corner of the barn, knelt and started to pray. I smiled at the sight of him putting his young faith into practice. His idea seemed to be the best of all, but I would have to say my prayer silently as I wrestled with the tiny lamb still lodged inside of its mother. As I worked to ease my hand into the mother sheep, the instrumental theme of the old television show, "Mission: Impossible," flashed through my mind.

With Janelle maintaining her hold on the sheep, I thrust my hand in as far and as hard as I could, desperately trying to grasp the lamb's leg. Even as I did this, I felt certain the unmoving lamb was dead, but the ewe's life was also in jeopardy. I feared that my efforts would prove futile. The position I had to get into was awkward and off-balance, and could not seem to gain enough leverage to free the lamb's foreleg and pull it out.

Nearly resigned to giving up and accepting the

situation as hopeless, I noticed Jim out of the corner of my eye. I was amazed by the intensity of how he was praying. Every so often he would pause, glance at the unfolding drama, and ask, "How's it going, Dad?" Then he would resume his prayerful posture.

Even Janelle had gotten caught up in the excitement and suspense of the moment. She had long since forgotten about her unfinished homework that lay in her room awaiting her return. And her normally independent spirit had been pushed aside temporarily as we worked together in tandem—she bracing the ewe, Jim filling the role of prayer warrior, and me persistently pushing and pulling (and hoping for the best).

Not wanting to disappoint my eager and expectant offspring, I made one additional thrust with my arm. Eureka! I suddenly had managed a firm grip on one leg. As quickly as possible, I worked the leg out of the womb alongside the head. Within seconds the lamb slid out cleanly and easily, as if there had never been a problem.

To our dismay, the lamb lay still on the barn floor, showing no evidence of life. More strongly than ever, I suspected that it was dead, but just in case I tapped it on its side—and it coughed! All of us (even the ewe, I believe) heaved a sigh of relief. In spite of her very recent travail, the adult sheep quickly followed her instincts to begin her motherly chores.

We watched this incredible scene for a minute or two, assured that both momma and baby were now out of danger. Certain that we had done all that we could do, I suggested, "Kids, let's leave her alone with the lamb," and herded Jim and Janelle—with elated smiles filling their faces—back to the house. It seemed that staying to watch the mother clean up her lamb and get it moving around would be anticlimactic to the miracle in which we had just taken part.

We also had some cleaning up to do. If we hurried, I urged the kids, there still was enough time to change our clothes, eat and drive to church. Fortunately, Ardie had prepared some meals for us in advance, so all we had to do was warm them up for our supper. And it seemed appropriate to proceed to church and express our thanks to God for enabling us to help those pitiful animals.

Less than thirty minutes later we were ready, with fresh clothes and full stomachs. Before leaving, we decided to stop by the barn once more to see how the ewe and the newborn were coming along. To our shock, this miracle had taken on even greater significance: Over the brief span of time that we were away, the ewe had borne a second lamb! (No wonder things had been so snug for the first one.) Happily, for lamb No. 2 there had been no complications, and we were able to rejoice over having been participants in the birth of twin lambs.

This special moment is forever etched in our memories. I had survived my first (and as it turned out, only) attempt as a sheep midwife. The wonder of birth was impressed indelibly upon each of us. We had succeeded without the help of the "pros"—Ardie, my neighbor, even the veterinarian. God's help had proved sufficient. My son's prayers had been answered so vividly. In the years since, this experience for both Jim and Janelle served to confirm their belief in the God who created all we see and touch. They also have gained a greater, more profound appreciation for the gift of life.

This also presented us with a powerful lesson in perseverance. Sometimes in life there is no choice of alternatives, no "plan B." You just have to do what you think is right, as well as you possibly can, and trust that things will work out for the best with God's help. It would have been easy for us to give up, resigning ourselves to the seeming futility of trying to free the lamb from its mother's womb. I'm grateful that we didn't quit but determined to keep trying, because it would have cost not only the lives of the ewe and the trapped lamb, but also its twin.

At this point, let me offer a little disclaimer: Events like this one were hardly the norm during the fourteen years I shepherded our flock of about twenty sheep. If you feel inspired to produce a reality TV show on the life and times of sheep, I guarantee that for the most part it would be pretty boring. But we dealt with an endless stream of problems, even if none reached the magnitude of a lamb stuck in limbo during labor. Often these experiences also left memorable impressions, showing in many ways that, like it or not, people truly are very much like these lovable, generally hapless creatures.

Because of the insights I have gained during this process of serving as sheep caretaker, I am no longer surprised when I come across passages in the Bible that utilize the sheep theme to communicate an important principle. Both the Old and New Testaments are sprinkled with sheep analogies. For example, in an Old Testament book we find this statement: "For thus says the Lord God, 'Behold, I myself will search for My

11

sheep and seek them out. As a shepherd cares for his flock in the day when he is among his scattered sheep, so I will care for My sheep and will deliver them from all the places to which they were scattered on a cloudy and gloomy day" (Ezekiel 34:11-12). Wow, how I can identify with the idea of delivering sheep on a cloudy and gloomy day!

I had been reading the Bible for a number of years before I began the process of becoming acquainted with sheep "up close and personal." It was exciting to see the Scriptures come alive in my daily dealings with these mild-mannered mammals. But even better, I have been amazed to discover that many of the principles that I learned among the sheep also apply to other areas of life, such as family life, relationships and work.

We will unfold many of these insights over the following chapters, but I recall another time when prayer and teamwork helped to give birth—in this instance, to a new idea.

It was 1970, a time when the business world looked very different from how it looks today. My managerial responsibilities were fairly simple and straightforward, at least on paper. All I had to do was see to it that commercial and residential telephone service was maintained without disruption. This, as it turned out, was another example of a mission impossible. This was a year when Northwestern Bell was plagued by aging, tired equipment. There always seemed to be something breaking down. As you might imagine, we rarely heard from our customers unless they lost service unexpectedly. This particular year many of them chose to remain in frequent contact with us. It was amazing the amount of energy and determination they would exert to convey their conviction that properly functioning telephones are an inalienable right.

Because of the unusually large and ongoing volume of repair work we were performing, it seemed logical to me to hire a dispatcher to coordinate the response time of repair crews to trouble areas. Until that time, our trouble analysts also had coordinated repair assignments. The result, particularly during times of high demand, was a disjointed, inefficient operation. Too many times our repair crews crisscrossed in response to problem calls around the city. This consumed additional time, further delaying our ability to restore disrupted service.

Hiring a full-time dispatcher was a new concept that I felt was desperately needed. I also knew that for this proposal to gain acceptance, it would require careful presentation to union representatives—especially since I felt it might best be assigned to a woman, given the detailed and relational aspects of the job. Today such considerations might seem irrelevant, but this was years before any mention of the women's movement and efforts to secure gender equity in the workplace. Our union was very aggressive in seeking to preserve jobs as they were, which included a determination not to give new work to women. At the same time, there was valid concern about whether men working on the outside would resist a plan requiring that they take orders from a woman dispatcher.

We had to implement this idea, I was convinced, but how to do it without major disruption to employee/ employer relations at that time? As my idea took form,

I determined that the dispatching of repair crews could be coordinated by using an electronic display board with multiple sets of red and green lights controlled from one panel. Red would mean there was trouble in an area with no available repairmen. Green would indicate there was trouble, but a repair crew was on the scene. The dispatcher would pinpoint trouble areas on the map, illuminate a red light on the board to identify that area of the city, and wait until the nearest repairmen became available. This plan seemed simple enough. The question was whether the workers would accept it.

My first step was to pray about this problem and my proposed solution. I asked God to give me wisdom in how to communicate the severity of the situation and the remedy that I wanted to recommend. Then I explained the idea to my staff. I wanted to involve them in the solution and solicit their suggestions on how to proceed. A member of our crew who enjoyed carpentry as a hobby volunteered to build the display board. Another technician whose pastime was electronics stepped up and offered to do the wiring for the board. Several other men contributed to the project in various ways.

In the end, we had succeeded together in developing an efficient new method for promptly and efficiently dispatching our repair crews. We then selected one of the top women clerks in the office to serve as the dispatcher.

The day we turned on the new system, everything went smoothly. There were times when some of the outside service workers would complain about the dispatching method, but union leaders defended the project since they had been directly involved in its development and implementation. Our system was later written up in a prominent trade journal, and at least one railroad line adapted our display board for its uses.

During those days I realized how being a leader, whether in the home or in business, is very similar to being a shepherd. You have to demonstrate your concern for your "sheep," and it's important to demonstrate that you are trustworthy. Once that is established, it really isn't hard to be an effective leader.

Over the next chapters, we will be considering some specific principles about life and leadership that we can learn from sheep and shepherding. To get us started, let's take a look at the sometimes irresistible lure of the grass that is "greener" on the other side of the fence.

THOUGHTS TO CONSIDER AND DISCUSS:

1. Who are the lambs in your life for whom you are responsible? (See John 21:15, where Jesus tells Peter to "feed my lambs.")

   Jake, Matt, my Mom & Dad Bible Study Group,

2. Think of a time when your "circuits" – whether at home or at work – seemed ready to go into overload. Did you feel you were being asked to do more than you were able to handle? How did you cope with that situation? What does Philippians 4:13 ("I can do all things through Christ who strengthens me") have to say about circumstances like this?

   Pray - Seek Counsel

3. What role does prayer have in your life today? Be honest with your answer. When faced with a crisis, why is it that we often regard prayer as our "last resort"? When 1 Thessalonians 5:17 tells us to "pray without ceasing," how does that relate to you in practical terms – if at all?

   #1 Priority to pray for every one & every thing.

16

Chapter Two:
THE GRASS IS ALWAYS GREENER - OR SO IT SEEMS!

"Then the lambs will graze as in their pasture...."
– Isaiah 5:17

My decision to enter the world of shepherding or sheep-raising, as I mentioned earlier, was not the fulfillment of a lifelong dream. In fact, while it was not the farthest thing from my mind, I think it was in that general vicinity. Actually, my 14-year adventure in caring for sheep happened almost by accident.

Ardie had grown up on a farm, but after we got married she had graciously endured being separated from the rural lifestyle that she had loved so much. Like many people in corporate life, we found that my career with Northwestern Bell required frequent relocations. Finally, after being transferred from one city in Minnesota to another, we had an opportunity to move to the "Twin Cities"—the Minneapolis/St. Paul area. Ardie was just as enthused about this move as I was, but made one stipulation: She wanted us to find a house in the country, away from the city. She was living proof that you can take the farm girl off of the farm, but you can't get the farm out of the farm girl.

So when I accepted my new assignment in Northwestern Bell's St. Paul office, we quickly started searching for our rural home. It wasn't long before we found some farmland that pleased both of us. The only problem was that it consisted of forty acres, and we could not afford to buy that much property—nor could we maintain that much land. When we explained this to the real estate agent, he asked how many acres we thought we could afford. His question surprised us, because we knew that generally it is easier for a realtor to sell a parcel of land in one piece rather than breaking it into smaller tracts that might offer less buyer appeal. However, with his help in negotiating, we worked out an arrangement to buy twenty-four acres. Suddenly, Ardie and Ken Johnson had a "farm," our very own.

The next question was a very practical one: What should we do with it? Our initial plan was to cultivate a very sizable garden and acquire some animals for our children to care for, perhaps as a 4-H project. We did already have one animal on site, a horse that came with the farm. He seemed like a nice horse, but since I had not spent much time around horses, I wasn't a very good judge. If you had asked me what kind of horse he was, I would have replied with great certainty, "A brown one." (I later learned it was an Arabian.)

Wanting to live in some degree of harmony with our neighbors, we determined that grazing animals would help to keep the grass and weeds at a respectable height. The alternative was a tractor or a very speedy mower, and neither held much attraction for me. The first animals we tried were pigs, but they discouraged us quickly. They were very destructive, breaking windows and doors in the barn, and the existing fences did not seem to slow them very much. It was hard to catch them and a dirty task to feed them. Pigs presented lots of negatives, and no real positives that we could see.

Eventually we got rid of the four pigs—all females—by selling them to my brother-in-law, Howard. He also had a farm, but was far more experienced in raising and caring for hogs, so we thought it was a good trade-off. It was—for Howard. Over the next several years our reject hogs more than paid off his investment, presenting him with more than $10,000 worth of baby pigs.

Having gotten the pigs out of our system, we turned to Plan B: Chickens. Unfortunately, they also proved to more trouble than they were worth to us. Feeding costs were high, they really weren't much help in maintaining the grass and weeds, and we found that chickens did not hold much appeal for our children. Have you ever tried hugging a chicken?

When we had opted to try chickens, we actually had counted on the benefit of some experience—that is, Ardie's experience. She had helped her parents raise chickens when she was a girl, but had not always been successful. She vividly recalls the first time she tried to kill a chicken for dinner: Her mother usually performed the task, so following the steps she remembered from watching her mother, Ardie attempted to coax the chicken to lay its neck across a log. Holding the chicken with one hand, she raised the ax, swung, and cut off the bird's beak! I understand the bird never clucked the same after that.

After eliminating pigs and chickens, we felt we

were running out of choices. The weather was a major factor in our decision to settle on sheep. During our third summer at the farm, we were in the midst of a drought. It had hardly rained for weeks and because of the shortage of water, the grass in all the pastures in our area grew very slowly. As a result, after animals had grazed on some acreage for a while, it became depleted for the remainder of the season. Then there was no alternative but to relocate them to a new section of pasture.

Toward the end of the summer, our neighbor to the east had run out of pastureland for his sheep and asked if he could use some of our acreage. Our pastures weren't being used, so we were happy to oblige him and his flock. We thought nothing more about it, but as the summer drew to a close, the neighbor felt he owed us something to compensate for the use of our land. "Payment" came in the form of several lambs. Since we still had not settled on what kind of animals to raise on our farm, we accepted them.

Thus we became owners of several fuzzy, cuddly little sheep. Being a city boy, I didn't know any more about sheep than I knew about our other "test animals," but thankfully Ardie did. Her family had also raised sheep on their farm, so she was delighted by the new additions to our farm.

I never could have imagined how much our sheep would teach us over the next fourteen years. While Ardie had the experience, it became my assignment to gain on-the-job training in their care and feeding. The first thing I discovered was how enjoyable they were to have around. Compared to the pigs that had behaved most of the time like rebellious teenagers, the sheep were more like innocent babies, totally dependent on us and appreciative of everything that we did for them. From the start I began to recognize striking similarities between sheep—and humans. For instance, I learned that people are not the only species that seems convinced that the grass is greener on the other side of the fence.

Several seasons passed and we found ourselves in the midst of another dry, hot summer—much like the one when we received our first lambs. By the end of the summer, nourishing blades of grass in our pasture had become as scarce as five-leaf clovers. The sheep, of course, did not understand. They just knew they were hungry and wanted something to eat. "Do something!" they seemed to be thinking whenever I was around them.

In desperate need of pastureland, we devised a plan to turn our large side yard next the house into a temporary pasture. It covered nearly an acre and could accommodate our little flock for at least several weeks. We realized that if a landscaping specialist were to happen by, cardiac arrest could likely follow, but given the circumstances, we were willing to assume that risk. Aesthetics had to be secondary to the feeding and well-being of our sheep.

To create this "instant pasture," we erected a temporary fence that would keep the sheep confined and prevent them from getting close enough to eat the flowers and shrubs Ardie had so carefully and lovingly cultivated. Even though the fence would exist only as an interim part of our lawn décor, we made certain it was firmly in place before bringing in our flock, which by that time numbered twenty sheep. Since sheep have an annoying habit of pushing or bumping into fences or any other barrier, permanent or short-term, we knew the side yard enclosure could not be haphazardly erected.

It took several hours to erect the four-foot fence that consisted of seven horizontal woven-wire strands, interwoven with vertical strands to keep them stationary. The rectangular holes between the strands were smallest at the bottom to prevent lambs from sneaking through, and wider at the top since even adult sheep could not climb through at that height.

When we had completed the job, we let the sheep into the fresh, new pasture area, never before touched by wooly lambs. As soon as we opened the gate, the sheep scampered in excitedly and began checking out their new surroundings. Before long they were busily chomping on the new grass, quickly forgetting that they had just entered territory that only minutes before had been reserved as off-limits for them. Never doubting that their shepherd had arranged for a sumptuous meal, they began snapping off one blade of grass after another and contentedly chewing away.

Our hard labors finished, my family retreated to the house for our reward, a hearty lunch. We felt good about what we had accomplished and commended each other's contributions to the effort. Midway through the meal I got up to get something and happened to glance out the window toward the makeshift pasture. What I saw was unforgettable.

Across the yard, lined up closely together along the new fence, stood each of the twenty sheep. They all had their heads jutting through the fence strands, and almost in tandem were pushing and straining against the fence to reach the blades of grass farthest from them. I felt thankful that we had insisted on erecting a strong, sturdy fence, because I could see the muscles in their rear legs tensed with the strain of extending as far as possible to reach what lay on the other side of the boundary.

Of course, they had barely touched the grass that they had ready access to on the side yard. But even though they had more than enough grass on their side of the fence to keep them busy for many days, apparently the grass on the opposite side appeared greener and more enticing. We marveled at how a simple barrier could make identical sections of grass look so different. Apparently none of the sheep had bothered to consider if it might have been easier—and less strenuous—to simply ingest the grass they were trampling beneath their feet.

If I had taken a photo of this scene, the caption surely would have written itself: "The grass is always greener on the other side of the fence." I could hardly believe the sight of these sheep, so intent upon attaining the unattainable. Rather than being coined by some literary immortal, I imagine the "grass is greener" adage probably had its roots in the observations of some wise, old shepherd who had grown accustomed to the foibles of his flock over many years. One reason sheep so often get themselves into trouble is due to their insistence on trying to get what they cannot have.

Sound like anyone you know? I think we all have personal knowledge of greener-grass thinking in a variety of ways. Someone's marriage seems happier and more satisfying than ours. Another family's children seem more well-behaved, even smarter than ours. We were perfectly content with our car, until a friend bought one that seemed so much nicer. And our house? Well, if we could just have one like the So-and-so's!

I spent much of my time consulting with business owners and executives, and the "greener grass syndrome" seems to be a particularly powerful seduction for those of us who spend so many of our hours and days immersed in the work world. A different career seems more exciting than the one we already have. A competing company appears to offer a better working environment, not to mention better pay and benefits. Even within our own businesses, someone else's department seems to run far more productively and efficiently than our own.

For the past 14 years, I have led a ministry to business owners and top leaders called Christian Network Teams or simply, CNT. Our approach is to provide Christian executives a peer group that can provide them with wise, godly counsel on a monthly basis.

It has been my great joy and privilege to become deeply acquainted with hundreds of leaders who are genuinely committed to serving Jesus Christ through their companies and organizations. These small accountability groups are very helpful for keeping them on track in their determination to be effective representatives of the Lord in the marketplace. I have noticed a few times, however, when the lure of the greener grass has outweighed the influence of the CNT group.

I recall a very successful business owner, I'll call

him Doug, who was in one of our CNT groups some years back. He truly was a gifted leader and had made a considerable impact in his company—and in his community—for the Lord. Despite the success of his business, however, Doug began feeling restless. He longed for some fresh, new challenges.

The answer, Doug determined, was to start expanding his company and diversify into other areas. This would reenergize his entrepreneurial spirit and, he reasoned, broaden the impact of his company's Christian witness. Fellow members of his CNT group appreciated his eagerness, but cautioned him against taking on more than he could handle. Doug's can-do spirit was not to be denied, however, and soon his expansion and diversification plans were well underway.

Warnings he had received proved true as the additional business responsibilities began to demand more and more of his time. No matter how you slice it, a week has but 168 hours, so Doug began to cut back on other obligations to accommodate his increased workload. Although he bristled when anyone suggested it, he clearly had become overextended. Something had to go, and some things did. Commitments he had long valued, such as church and community activities, as well as his regular participation in his CNT group, were greatly curtailed or dropped.

Consumed by what many people have termed "the tyranny of the urgent," Doug began to lose sight of the important—those things that deserved a top priority in his life. Having to work long hours, starting early in the morning and continuing well into the evening, his spiritual life also took a hard hit. All because the attraction of becoming bigger and better, trying to keep pace with some of his competitors, had seduced him.

Sadly, Doug is not the rare exception. Over the years I have encountered many business owners with viable businesses that were profitable and growing, yet they itched to get started with another idea. Sometimes this means entering a totally new field of endeavor that consumes energy, financial resources and enthusiasm. Often this drama ends with both businesses in trouble, family relationships stretched to the breaking point, and an accumulation of pain that could never have been imagined.

A number of years ago, Ardie and I had a far less serious encounter with the "greener grass" that was both humorous and ironic. After moving from our native Minnesota to Tennessee in 1983, we relished the prospect of enjoying warm weather for much longer periods of time. In particular, we thought about how wonderful it would be to barbecue many of our meals on an outdoor grill—something residents of Minnesota rarely do.

The question was, what kind of grill should we use? As we deliberated about the grill of our dreams, we concluded that the old, black-domed charcoal model that we had used occasionally up north would not suffice. For barbecue perfection, we would need a propane-fueled gas grill! In our minds we could almost taste the difference in our steaks, chickens, hamburgers and hot dogs. (Out of respect for the sheep we had left behind, we omitted lamb chops from our projected menu.)

One day we commented to a neighbor about our interest in obtaining a gas grill. "That's a coincidence,"

26

she replied. "I have two grills. One is propane and the other is natural gas. I have been thinking about trying one of those black-domed, charcoal grills." We were amazed to discover the grass is even greener around the grill!

Thinking back to that time when our sheep lined up in tight formation along the fence, pushing to reach the grass on the opposite side, I had noticed an interesting side effect. Their straining was ruining the grass right beneath their feet, much more grass than they could reach on the fence's other side. Obviously, if our sheep could have stopped long enough to analyze their actions, they immediately would have realized how foolish and greedy they were. Analysis and common sense, however, are notoriously absent among sheep. They stubbornly proceed with blind determination, simply following their impulses.

It would be nice to think that sheep are unique in this shortcoming. The fact is, however, that human "sheep" sometimes are not much different—and sometimes even worse. In our relentless quest to obtain the greener grass, we can destroy some precious "turf" in the process.

Tom is an example who comes to mind. I knew him years ago, a highly successful professional man with the picture-perfect family. He did not seem to lack anything. He had a beautiful home, cars, nice clothes, prominence in his profession, and respect in his community. His life was the kind that many other people would perceive as the "greener grass."

For a number of months, Tom and I met regularly for breakfast or lunch to discuss common interests and concerns. In the process we became fairly good friends. As I got to know him, I was impressed by Tom's perspective on life. He seemed to understand the perils of excessive pride and the endless pursuit of personal gain. After a while, however, it became evident that he was a fence straddler, increasingly inclined to gaze longingly toward the enticing grass outside his own confines. Everything that he possessed on his own side of the fence suddenly seemed insufficient.

Tom began to yield to the temptations of more money, more prestige, and more self-gratification. Wealth is not necessarily wrong in itself, but this man clearly had become afflicted by what the Bible terms as "the love of money." Despite a prospering career that easily provided far more than he and his family could ever need, Tom felt a compelling desire to diversify into other businesses. He started by investing in a business venture that was totally unrelated to his profession, and then he excitedly jumped at an opportunity to engage in some time-consuming consulting work.

His personal tastes began to change, with material possessions rising dramatically on his scale of importance. Our friendship became weakened by the growing disparity between what he and I viewed as the significant, top-priority elements of life. While not wanting to judge his behavior, I still felt saddened because it was evident that the changes in my friend were not for the better.

Eventually, the greener grass expanded to include more than business pursuits and just "stuff." He became intimately involved with another woman, his marriage disintegrated, and he lost forever the adoration of his wife and children. In time the "other woman" faded from the scene, but by that time the damage was irreparable. Many of his business investments failed, adding financial pressures to his personal pain. His once promising life turned into a terrible tragedy, and it was all so unnecessary. Sometimes when I think about this man, I can almost picture him as one of my silly sheep, with his head thrust through a temporary fence, greedily groping for grass that somehow appears greener.

I think we can agree that one of the greatest devices for perpetuating the greener grass myth is TV. I enjoy watching good TV shows from time to time, but so many of the commercials and much of the programming content seem tailored to tantalize us with whatever we do not have, rather than deepening our appreciation for what we already do have. After spending a few hours watching TV, we can sometimes find it difficult to distinguish our "wants" from our needs. Even if we have a nice car, TV commercials introduce us to a better one. We might have a perfectly functional computer, but TV entices us with a faster, more powerful one. TV even tries to persuade us to buy bigger, higher-definition TVs, for goodness sake!

This is probably why one of the Ten Commandments instructs us, "Do not covet." In sheep language, this means, "even though it may seem to be so, the grass on the other side of the fence really isn't any greener."

I'd be remiss if I didn't make mention of another side to this fence issue—no pun intended. While observing my sheep over the years, they taught me that while fences can and generally do restrict our access to whatever surrounds us, they also can provide security and a sense of peace.

Whenever our sheep were turned out to an

unfamiliar area, their initial reaction was to act skittish. They would act fearful of the slightest commotion, and usually stood in one place until they could locate where the fence was. Once they had clearly identified their new borders, the sheep would settle down and resume their normal routine. It was interesting that one part of their nature urged them to reach for what they could see beyond the fence, while another part found comfort in the protection of the fence. Disturbances outside the fence did little to disrupt their tranquility—as long as everything remained calm within their own boundaries.

I have discovered this same principle applies to the family—and in large measure, the workplace. One reason children disobey, experts tell us, is to test their boundaries. It's not that they resent or reject the boundaries—they just want to clarify where they are so they can operate freely within those limits. Dr. James Dobson, a prominent authority on the family, writes in his book, *Dr. Dobson Answers Your Questions:*

When a child behaves in ways that are disrespectful or harmful to himself or others, his hidden purpose is often to verify the stability of the boundaries...a child who assaults the loving authority of his parents is greatly reassured when their leadership holds firm and confident. He finds his greatest security in a structured environment where the rights of other people (and his own) are protected by definite boundaries.[1]

In our marriage, Ardie and I have found that our relationship works in a similar way. I can remember Ardie saying to me a number of times, especially while

---

[1] *Dr. Dobson Answers Your Questions,* by James Dobson, © 1982, Word Books, Waco, Texas, p. 120.

our children were growing up, "I want to know where my fences are." She was referring to my expectations for her, such as how much money she could spend without our needing to schedule a husband-wife consultation. Once she had that framework, she could confidently carry out her responsibilities for the home and our children without risking conflict with me. Being called by God to provide leadership in our home, I would have been shirking this responsibility by failing to offer those guidelines. At the same time, since our marriage is a true partnership, I have always asked Ardie to help me to identify my own "fences" from her perspective.

The application for a workplace setting is obvious. An employee usually works most effectively when he or she clearly understands the work responsibilities, knows the degree of freedom permitted in carrying out the job, has been informed of the employer's expectations, and has been apprised of other parameters that pertain to the tasks to be done.

So while our "fences" can often seem like an annoyance, keeping us from the grass that seems so much more lush and green than what we find right under our feet, they also provide considerable benefit. If we're honest, in most cases we don't want to have our fences taken down; we just like to test them from time to time. Do you or those who work with you sometimes wrestle with anxiety and insecurity? Maybe the solution could be a friendly, reassuring fence!

Next we will look at some insights that the sheep taught me about a familiar children's game, "Follow the leader," that we frequently see also being conducted in various ways in our everyday world.

THOUGHTS TO CONSIDER AND DISCUSS:

1. Recall an experience in your life – a possible job change, a different home, a new car, etc. – when the "grass" seemed greener elsewhere, but later you discovered that your own "pasture" was as good or better. What made the alternative seem so appealing at the time?

2. Is there an area of your life now when you find yourself gazing longingly at the "greener grass"? How can you evaluate your options most effectively, and accurately? What part does honoring God have in your considerations? When Matthew 6:33 tells us to "seek first His kingdom and His righteousness," how can that affect the decisions we make?

3. What brings security into your life? And what things seem to threaten that security? In a world filled with uncertainty, insecurity and instability, how can we experience lives that feel stable and secure? Look up Isaiah 41:10 and consider what it has to say about these concerns.

Chapter Three:
LET'S PLAY FOLLOW THE LEADER

"The Lord is my shepherd...He leads me beside quiet waters." – Psalm 23:1-2

One chilly morning the alarm clock roused me out of my wintry hibernation. Mustering the determination of a fullback fighting for the final yard into the end zone, I forced myself out of bed to greet another day. Instantly feeling the nip in the air, I briefly entertained a temptation to crawl back under the covers, but thinking about the busy day ahead convinced me to move into action.

After showering and shaving, I slid into my coveralls and headed for the barn to tend to the sheep. As I opened the barn door and called to them, I grabbed a hoe to do a quick cleanup just outside the entrance. I could hear the sluggish sheep moving about, beginning their parade toward the doorway.

Acting on a playful impulse, I took the hoe handle and held it in front of the first ewe, about knee high, as she started out the door. Instead of being stopped by the obstacle, she gracefully leaped over the stick and proceeded, without any hesitation, toward the pasture.

I pulled the hoe handle away before the second sheep got to the door, but was fascinated to see what happened next. One after another, each of the remaining twenty sheep came to where the first ewe had jumped – and duplicated the feat! As if on command, each sheep launched itself into the air at that precise spot, completed its jump, and then fell in step with the animal directly in front of it.

As you can imagine, it was a curious sight. The fact that the original motivation for jumping – the hoe handle – had been removed did not seem to concern the little flock of sheep in the slightest. All they knew was that the sheep immediately in front had jumped, and that seemed reason enough for doing the same. In fact, the last sheep jumped higher than any of the others.

That was years ago, but I can still picture those foolish sheep following one another's lead unquestioningly. It reminded me of a game we used to play when I was a boy, called "Follow the Leader." Perhaps you played it too. The rules were simple: The leader would perform a series of actions or stunts, and we would repeat them, one by one. These could include parading along the sidewalk, going up and down stairs, jumping, running, walking, even crawling. We followed the leader because we wanted to do so.

As adults, we sometimes find ourselves playing Follow the Leader as well, even though that may not be our intention. I saw this illustrated at a civic club luncheon I attended some time ago. The meeting began at noon, which does not seem particularly unusual, except this particular organization had opened its luncheons at 12:10 p.m. for as long as anyone could remember. Then a new club president was elected, obviously a real troublemaker and no respecter of tradition. One of his first official actions was to question the customary starting time, since most other local clubs began their activities promptly at noon.

No one could explain why this club's starting time was always ten minutes past noon. The best answer anyone could provide was, "Well, we have always done it that way." When the new president suggested changing the meeting time to noon, no one objected. In fact, some members wondered aloud why that decision had not been made sooner. (No one bothered to ask why 12 o'clock has become generally accepted as the official lunch hour, but that is a broader issue for another time – and probably another book.)

This reminds me of a man whose wife suffered from another classic example of "follow the leader syndrome." Whenever she prepared a ham for dinner, she had the unusual habit of cutting off both ends of the ham before putting it into the oven. After observing her do this on numerous occasions, the husband's curiosity finally could not be squelched. There may be a good reason for doing that, he thought, but it seemed like a waste of good meat. Finally he asked, "Honey, why do you cut the ends off the ham before you cook it and throw them away?"

"That's the way Mother always cooked our hams when I was growing up," his wife responded.

Her answer seemed reasonable, but it failed to ease his perplexity. All he could think about was the pounds of seemingly good meat that had been discarded over the years. The question, "Why?" still loomed.

The next time he saw his mother-in-law, the husband could hardly wait to ask her the same question. "Mom, Lil always cuts both ends off our hams just before she puts them in to cook. She says she learned that from you. I was just wondering – why do you do it?" The mother-in-law kindly replied, "That was also the way my mother cooked her hams when I was growing up."

Fortunately, Grandma was still living, so the great ham investigation did not end there. At the next family gathering, the still-curious husband was ready to pose his question once more. "Grandma, Lil always cuts off both ends of the ham before putting it in to cook. She learned it from her mom, and her mom says she learned it from you. Why did you do it?"

With a twinkle in her eyes, Grandma smiled and leaned toward her grandson-in-law, as if to share a secret of the ages. "You see, in our home in those days, I had just one little cooking pan, and the only way I could fit a ham into it was to cut off both ends first!"

In business, this follow-the-leader mindset can present serious problems. You may relate to a situation like this: A veteran manager leaves the company after a number of years and a new boss arrives, overflowing with new ideas and innovations. Almost immediately, he encounters resistance. "Well, Ms. Smith never did it that way. Would you like me to show you how she used to do it?"

Rapidly advancing, ever-changing technology seems particularly troublesome for anyone who enjoys the comfort of old, familiar ways. A new computer, data processing or records-keeping system may offer much greater speed and efficiency, but frequently our first reaction reflects our lack of confidence. "Our old way has served us long and faithfully. It still works. Why reinvent the wheel?" we complain, at least to ourselves.

We lapse into following the leader in many other ways. I have lost count of how many times I have gone to the back of a long line at a bank or in a grocery store, only to discover moments later that a teller or cashier is waiting at the other end without any customers at all. And if you happen to pass someone on the street who is staring upward, aren't you tempted to look up, too?

Advertising, whether it appears on TV, radio, newspapers or other media, employs – you might even say, abuses – "follow the leader" psychology. Well-known celebrities appear in commercials, informing us that they use specific brands of toothpaste, shampoo or deodorant, or wear special lines and styles of clothing. Soon we "sheep" go flocking to the stores to purchase those products, simply because some famous "leader" has told us to do so.

I have to admit that following the leader has sometimes proved embarrassing for me. There was a time, for example, when I was led astray, not by a flock of sheep but by a herd of cows. While Ardie and I were dating, I sometimes would join her at her parents' farm in Sandstone, Minnesota. By that time, the Swansons were raising cattle, having given up on trying to raise sheep and still manage to remain solvent.

On one of my first visits to the farm, Ardie decided I would benefit from an elementary lesson in working with cows. Because of the farm's terrain, it required a lot of land for all of the cows to graze. That usually meant a long walk at milking time, through brushland and woods, over and around streams, to round up the cows and head them back toward the barn.

Bringing in the cows sounded easy to me, and I reasoned it would be a good way to make some positive points with both Ardie and her father, Albert. One evening I set out on my mission. I had to take a round-about route since the most direct way was blocked by a wide, deep stream. After following the stream for a considerable distance, I found a place where it narrowed enough to jump across.

I finally tracked down the cows, which were grazing lazily in a meadow. I didn't take long to get them moving and ambling toward home. As we entered the wooded area, some of the thirty cows moved out of my sight, but I could hear their hooves crunching through twigs and leaves.

To my surprise, when the cows in front of me reached the stream, they opted for the shortcut, swimming across easily. Even though the creek was about fifteen feet wide, they had no problem crossing it. Not excited about retracing my earlier detour when I was searching for the cows, I wondered if there was not a way I could follow the animals by getting across the stream somehow. I noticed a limb from a nearby tree extending conveniently over the water. Surely, I thought, I can grab it and swing to the other side without getting wet.

I took hold of the limb and swung forward, doing my best Tarzan impersonation. Halfway across the stream, unfortunately, the limb snapped and deposited me unceremoniously into the water. Although the water was several feet over my head, I quickly returned to the surface and swam to the opposite bank.

Pulling myself out of the stream, I found that every bit of me – including my wallet and boots – was thoroughly soaked. Despite the setback, I felt pleased. I had succeeded in gathering the cows together and kept up with them as they trudged back to the barn. I anticipated a favorable appraisal of my performance from Ardie and her father.

My self-satisfaction was quickly squashed, however, as I spotted Ardie standing atop a nearby hill and I heard her shout, "Ken, you don't have all the cows!"

So much for words of encouragement! My first impulse was to yell back, "Forget the cows!" but I knew that was not the correct response. Dutifully I retraced my steps, taking the long but dry course, to find and herd the remaining bovine fugitives into the barn.

Later, Ardie's father offered this fair assessment: "Ken, I don't believe you'll ever make a good farmer, but then, I'd probably never make a good phone man."

Thankfully, Ardie was able to overlook my little escapade with the cows, and she married me two years later.

Fast-forwarding again to our hobby farm in rural St. Paul, I found it interesting to observe that sheep don't have to learn how to follow the leader. They do it instinctively, practically from birth. Any shepherd (traditional or part-time variety) enjoys watching new lambs in the first days of "freedom" from the barn. Since our lambs always were born while it was still cold, we kept them confined in the barn with their mothers until warmer days arrived. That meant each lamb's "world" for the first weeks of its life pretty much consisted of a pen with the dimensions of about five feet by five feet. Even for a lamb that is not much space, especially when it must be shared with "mom."

When warm weather finally arrived, we would send the ewes into the pastures with their lambs. The immediate surprise and delight of the little ones was obvious. They would romp into the open spaces, expending months of pent-up energy. After a quick glance to make sure their mothers were not far away, the lambs would gather in a group to play.

The pasture became a playground paradise for them. They would scamper happily from one side to another, rolling and tumbling in the fresh grass, running as fast as their little legs would permit. After a while they would pause on one side of the pasture, taking a brief rest. Suddenly one lamb would break for the opposite side and almost as quickly, the other lambs would follow in earnest pursuit.

As the lambs explored the pasture and their expanded world, they often would discover a tiny hill. One lamb would decide to become "king of the hill" until his friends came to join him. It was comical to see fifteen lambs each squirming for space on the hill, in their own way refuting the adage that it is always lonely at the top. For them, lonely no, but crowded yes! After standing still for a few moments, the lambs would look at each other as if to ask, "What do we do now?" Almost instantly, a lamb would charge off the hill, making a beeline for another section of the pasture. The others again would eagerly follow. They did not know where they were going, but they were determined not to be left behind.

Reflecting on these and other similar experiences, I am amazed how much we are like those little lambs as we go about our daily activities. Many of our established, revered traditions today continue long after their original purposes have ceased to exist. For instance, many churches have regular Sunday night services in addition to morning worship. I wholeheartedly support this practice, but do you know how Sunday evening services got started? Believe it or not, it was not because someone determined that one Lord's Day service was not enough.

Actually, the credit must go to the dynamic duo of evangelism – and gas lights! In the early nineteenth century, gas lights were too expensive for most private homes. As a result, people were fascinated by this new innovation and flocked to public buildings where the artificial illumination could transform night into day. Seeking to capitalize on this curiosity, ministers in many churches had gas lights installed in the sanctuaries and began to conduct Sunday evening services. While church members were encouraged to attend, the late services were designed to attract unchurched members of their communities and give them an opportunity to hear the gospel message.[2]

More than 150 years later, thousands upon thousands throng to their churches on Sunday nights, but most are totally unaware of the original intent for those meetings.

We could cite many other examples of tried-and-true traditions that have long since lost sight of their cause for existence, but having acknowledged our sheeplike "follow the leader" tendencies, I believe we can learn two important concepts.

---

[2] *The Seven Last Words of the Church,* by Ralph Neighbor, © 1973, Zondervan Publishing House, Grand Rapids, Michigan.

First of all, we need to become more wary of the "I don't want to try anything new" attitude that can cripple progress – in a company, a home, a church, or even a community. Many traditions are certainly deserving of being maintained, but it might not hurt to question established practices to ascertain whether they are still worth keeping. A few probing questions could help: "Why are we doing it this way?" "Is there a better, more effective approach?" "Does this have a real purpose, or are we just clinging to a comfortable old habit?"

Some years ago I learned an important business principle you might also be familiar with; it's called "going outside the nine dots." As you see in the diagram, there are nine dots in the shape of a square, lined up in rows of three. The challenge is to connect the nine dots by using only four lines – and not lifting your pen or pencil once you have started drawing the lines.

o   o   o

o   o   o

o   o   o

(Inc. magazine, March 1981, p. 143)

At first you puzzle over the problem, and may even conclude that the task cannot be done. If you restrict your thinking to staying within those nine dots, that is a correct analysis. No matter how you try, one or more dots will remain unconnected. However, if you extend your lines *outside* the nine dots, the puzzle can indeed be solved. (See page 47.)

Have you ever encountered a situation like that in the workplace? A problem occurs, and no solution seems to work. You agonize over your dilemma to no avail, partly because you are "following the leader" of ideas that have been used before. Then an associate suggests a solution that initially seems totally outside the realm of possibility. Very soon, however, you realize that while it is beyond the framework you had been working in, the proposed idea is perfectly acceptable. It is simply a fresh approach, completely different for what you had been considering. You shake your head as you reflect on this simple, innovative angle to the problem that had baffled you.

I remember a time when one of our Christian Network Team members faced such a dilemma. Because of a downturn in business that had resulted in a serious cash flow problem, Joe had to make a number of staff layoffs, hoping to rehire at least some of these people when sales improved. Not long afterward, his son, Brent, graduated from college. Joe had promised Brent a job with the company, but saw it as ethically wrong to hire a family member while other people's jobs were being eliminated. He also knew that how he handled the situation could affect his witness for Christ within the company.

Recognizing the value of wise counsel, Joe consulted with the other members of his CNT team. They agreed that while his decision not to hire his son would essentially be reneging on a promise, to bring the son on at a time when others were being laid off would severely compromise Joe's integrity as an employer.

The solution, one of his friends suggested, could be

to network with other company owners and try to find a suitable position for Brent. That idea excited Joe, and before long he succeeded in finding a different job for Brent that was an excellent fit for his college training and career goals. Ironically, months later Joe admitted, "Brent is probably doing better with the other company than if he had come to work with us!"

The second lesson I have learned from the members of my follow-the-leader flock is that we need to be sure we are following the right leader. Earlier I mentioned my less than successful experience with the cows. Years later, after I had become well-acquainted with the mannerisms of our sheep, I discovered that while cattle must be driven, a true shepherd leads his flock, showing the way and paying attention to how the sheep are faring

A friend once told me about an encounter he had in Israel that confirmed this. He was on a tour bus that came to a sudden halt while a man was shouting and forcing a flock of sheep to cross the roadway. "I thought that a shepherd leads his sheep, rather than driving them," my friend commented to the bus driver. "Oh, but sir," the driver replied, "that man is not a shepherd. He has only been hired to take these sheep to the market."

This "hireling" evidently had no personal connection with the sheep. His job was solely to get them from point A to point B. But just as a shepherd spends time with the sheep, observing and learning their behavior and quirks, a good leader mingles among the people he or she leads, getting to know them and how to lead them most effectively.

It is said that President Abraham Lincoln spent as

much as 75 percent of his time away from the White House during his first term in office. During the Civil War, the President's desire was to be with his troops, encouraging them and letting them know that he cared about them.

During my own management days with the telephone company, the term "MBWA" – management by walking around – gained a lot of attention, and I found it an effective strategy for understanding the needs and concerns of the men and women who worked for me. The information I gathered by simply walking around enabled me to make better decisions and provided needed encouragement for the employees, letting them know their leader was not distant and disinterested.

I remember an exit interview with an employee when I asked, as I always did, what she felt was the thing she had enjoyed most about working for our company. She commented it was the Monday morning walk-around that I did, taking the time to visit informally with the workers. I have to admit that until then I had not thought much about the impact I was making, it was just something I did that made sense. It was gratifying to hear how this practice had become a meaningful exercise for at least some of our people.

For believers, we know that ultimately the "right leader" to follow is Jesus Christ. He not only modeled how to live, but performed in the truest sense what today we often hear referred to as "the ultimate sacrifice." Speaking to His followers, He did not equivocate on the importance of their loyalty to Him as their shepherd. Jesus summed it up by saying, "If anyone wishes to come after Me, let him deny himself, and take up his cross daily, and follow Me" (Luke 9:23).

This declaration leaves little room for compromise. It is important to note that Jesus did not offer any exceptions to following Him, such as "except in business" or "except in certain personal situations," or "except when you have an option you like better."

Instead, He repeatedly points out that from His perspective we are sheep, just the human variety. He says he is "the good shepherd" (John 10:11). We have an assortment of shepherds to choose from, where we work and where we worship, but there is but one "good shepherd," Jesus asserts. We will look at some of the "alternative shepherds" in the next chapters.

THOUGHTS TO CONSIDER AND DISCUSS:

1. When was the last time you played "follow the leader"? What can you remember about that experience? What examples can you think of today in which society encourages us to continue following this pattern, even as adults?

2. We are all creatures of habit, to one degree or another. Think of an instance in your life when you have done something repetitively without ever asking, "Why?" Do you ever feel threatened by new ideas, or by breaking with old traditions and routines? Explain your answer.

3. What is a problem you are facing now that could best be resolved if you could go "outside the nine dots"? Isaiah 55:8 says that God's thoughts are not our thoughts, and His ways are not our ways. With this in mind, how might your relationship with God help you in finding an acceptable solution?

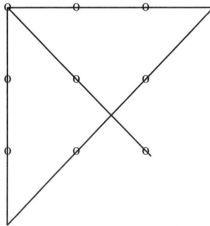

(The solution for connecting the nine-dots problem.)

Chapter Four:
YOU HAVE TO SET
A GOOD EXAMPLE

"My people have become lost sheep; their shepherds
have led them astray." – Jeremiah 50:6

When did you ever hear of an adult getting lost because he was following a child? I can't remember ever observing or being told about such a thing. An experienced shepherd knows the same is true of his flock. A mature sheep will not go off track by following a lamb; however, an adventuresome or disobedient ram or ewe can lead other members of the flock astray. One sheep following his nose toward the horizon that beckons in the distance can literally lead his companions down a path of destruction. A shepherd cannot afford to have that kind of "leader" in his flock.

What is a shepherd's recourse when he discovers a rebellious rascal in the midst of his flock? Sheep experts will advise you there is only one sure cure: Get rid of the troublemaker. This may seem harsh, but the well-being of the flock is worth far more than trying to cope with the repeated aggravations caused by a chronically bad example. At the same time, such

49

a decision should not be made in haste; you want to retain the sheep if at all possible.

Whenever I think about sheep like this – and we had a few during our fourteen years of shepherding – I am reminded of one of my favorite parables in the Bible. Jesus story in Matthew 18 about the "ninety and nine" actually focuses on one such headstrong, independent sheep, the one that strayed and became lost.

What do you think? If any man has a hundred sheep, and one of them has gone astray, does he not leave the ninety-nine on the mountains and go and search for the one that is straying? And if it turns out that he finds it, truly I say to you, he rejoices over it more than over the ninety-nine which have not gone astray (Matthew 18:12-13).

In this story, we see not only a shepherd's great love and devotion to each member of his flock, but also Christ's unlimited and unconditional love for His children. This parable many times has served as a wonderful source of assurance for me, reaffirming how important each one of us is to our Lord.

Jesus' parable, however, provides us with more than a generalized account of a wayward sheep. I believe it is significant that He spoke about an adult animal, rather than a lamb. This reminds us of the responsibility and influence we have on the "lambs" around us.

Lambs rarely venture very far from their mothers. In the last chapter, I told how the young lambs, even though they were enjoying their new freedom in the open pasture, always made sure to keep their moms in sight. That served two purposes: They maintained the sense of security they had enjoyed in the barn, and they also knew that when their internal dinner bells sounded, they were close to the "cafeteria."

An adult sheep is far more independent and generally can find his own food. It is when he wanders off, either in search of a more varied diet or to satisfy his curiosity, that he can stir up trouble – for himself and others. If he has some status in the flock and is accepted by his peers as a leader, you may soon have more than one lost sheep to track down.

Years ago, Thomas Spurgeon put the dilemma into verse:

'Twas a Sheep, Not a Lamb

It was a sheep – not a lamb, that strayed away,
In the parable Jesus told:
A grown-up sheep that had gone astray
From the ninety and nine in the fold.

Out in the meadows, out in the cold,
'Twas a sheep the good Shepherd sought.
Back to the flock and into the fold,
'Twas a sheep the good Shepherd brought.

And why for the sheep, should we earnestly long,
And so earnestly hope and pray?
Because there is danger, if they go wrong,
They will lead the young lambs away.

For the lambs follow the sheep, you know,
Wherever the sheep may stray;
If the sheep go wrong, it will not be long
Till the lambs are as wrong as they.

So with the sheep we earnestly plead,
For the sake of the lambs today.
If the lambs are lost, what a terrible cost,
Some sheep may have to pay!

Relating this to the human level, we don't have to think very long to list several examples of leadership that resulted in horrific tragedy. Adolf Hitler at one time was well-regarded; many German citizens unquestioningly followed his direction, even when his murderous objectives became evident. Because of that one "sheep," millions of men, women and children were led to the slaughter in the most literal sense.

More than 25 years have passed, but another unbelievable tragedy that many of us still remember involved the Rev. Jim Jones, who at first appeared to be a sincere man, dedicated to serving God. Years later, however, Jones assumed the role of his own god and led another holocaust, misguiding 913 people to their deaths in Jonestown, Guyana in 1978. We could fill the remainder of this book with a discussion of other monstrous personalities.

Of course, tragedies precipitated by wayward sheep can take other forms. In the business world, in the last decade we have seen the colossal demise of numerous companies and firms that once commanded great prominence and respect. Today, names like Enron and Arthur Anderson have fallen from admiration to corporate infamy. And much of the responsibility for these collapses rests on the shoulders of the top executives, the "sheep/shepherds," who led them. In these cases, the carnage may not be measured in physical death, but rather in shattered lives and devastated careers.

It's clear that these grim events from the recent and distant past serve as vivid examples of the consequences of following the wrong sheep. Equally important, these tragedies also demonstrate the great responsibility we carry whenever we have the privilege and opportunity to serve as shepherds or leaders for others.

In 1 Peter 5:2-3, we are exhorted to, "...shepherd the flock of God among you, not under compulsion, but voluntarily...proving to be examples to the flock." During my days as a shepherd, I discovered a secret to effective leadership: To guide the sheep, you need a "sheep magnet." This was not an actual magnet, of course, but rather a bucket of feed or water. Unlike human beings, sheep are not impressed by the externals of personal appearance, but a bucket that promises a treat – even one that is rusted or dented – generally gains a sheep's full attention.

Interestingly, after a while it is not the bucket's contents, but the mere promise of the contents, that lures the sheep. Once they have learned it may contain grain or water, even an empty bucket will bring them running. Any time I wanted to get my flock's attention, I would simply grab a bucket and rattle it a couple of times. It never failed to draw them to me.

Extending this process one step further, once the sheep have learned to associate the shepherd with the beckoning bucket, they start to readily follow the shepherd even when he does not have the bucket. A sense of trust and dependence has been established, and the sheep develop a close association with their leader.

Sheep – like people – occasionally need proper behavior reinforced if it is to continue. For this reason, from time to time I would let my sheep have the bucket instead of just dangling it in front of them. Often a sheep, in its enthusiasm to consume the grain, would stick its head deep into the bucket. Occasionally the handle would get caught around the sheep's neck and over its ears, sending the animal into a fit of perplexity and panic.

Sheep, not being a species known for powers of analysis, have no simple solution to the question, "What do you do when you have accidentally gotten the bucket handle caught around your neck?" The general response is to do what comes most naturally – run around the pasture in blind dismay and frustration. This may sound humorous, but if you think it is easy to catch and help a sheep in that condition, you should try it some day!

Again relating our principles to people, this concept of "bucket leadership" is relevant. To be a leader you need followers, and to have followers, you must offer something that is attractive and appealing. This is true for political parties, which offer specific platforms and ideologies for their loyal – and prospective – supporters. This type of lure also explains in large measure the fascination some people have with religious cults that promise to meet such foundational human needs as love, peace, acceptance, purpose, and a sense of belonging.

In the workplace, the quality of leadership frequently is the deciding factor in the success or failure of a project, not to mention the survival and growth of an entire company. While I was with the telephone company, one man particularly impressed me as a strong and able leader. Actually, he was my boss's boss, but I had the chance to observe him closely in action on many occasions. It was interesting that what made him most effective as a leader was not his ability to enforce his orders, but his obvious and sincere concern for people. It's a fact that people usually are most interested in someone who is interested in them. This man set high expectations and goals for his workers, and was very demanding, but he also was fair and supportive of his employees. The result? He received an extremely high level of loyalty and commitment from all of them.

As I advanced to take on new management responsibilities, this man's compassion and sensitivity served as a continuing example for me. One day in particular stands out for me. I had just been transferred from Cloquet, Minnesota to Duluth. These cities were just twenty miles apart, but we had an unusually heavy snow and there was no way for me to return home. Everything was at a standstill in the city for two days – that is, except for telephone problems, which not only continued but also intensified.

I had to get a room at a local hotel, but had not been prepared for an overnight stay. Without being asked, this executive – who was not even my immediate superior – brought me a clean shirt, toothbrush and razor. It was a simple act, and not particularly expensive, but his thoughtfulness left an indelible impression.

I have not always succeeded, but I've tried in similar ways to acknowledge extra effort by people who have worked for me. One winter, the telephone lines near Cloquet required some extensive and complicated circuitry work. The project had to be done during the night to avoid disrupting telephone service during the day and inconveniencing our users. I did not have to perform any of this work personally, but was responsible for supervising the project. We were living in the town at the time and it was a bitterly cold night, the kind that makes you especially thankful for a warm, well-insulated house. As I sat in the living room and looked through the window, I could see the snow blowing outside and hear the wind buffeting our house. On TV, the weatherman reported the temperature was 10 degrees below zero and advised, "It's a good night to stay inside and off the roads."

As he said that, an image flashed through my mind of the meager canvas enclosure that served as the only protection for one of the three-man crews working forty miles to the north. The mere thought of venturing into the cold caused me to shiver, but I felt the need to do something for the men to show my appreciation for their work under such adverse conditions. At the phone company our slogan was, "The Spirit of Service," and on that night the crew was living out that motto – and then some.

It was close to midnight, but I put on my coat and – after assuring Ardie that I was not suffering from frostbite of the brain – got into my car and drove to a restaurant in Cloquet to buy a bag of hamburgers for the men. It was the pre-McDonald's era, and I had the waitress pack the sandwiches tightly to keep them warm. Then I got back into my car and drove toward the frigid work site.

Technically, these men were not my crew and did

not report directly to me. They had been temporarily assigned to my area, but since I was in charge of this special project, I felt responsible for the men's well-being. When I arrived, the men looked puzzled. They had heard my car crunching along the snow-crusted roadway. The nearest town was twenty miles away and, understandably, there was not a lot of competing noise that evening. Since it was unlikely that anyone would be taking a leisurely drive at that hour and under those conditions, they could not imagine who was coming when they heard my car creak to a stop at the side of the road.

Trudging the short distance in the drifted snow, I announced, "Men, I've got some goodies for you!" They had not been expecting a delivery man from Hamburger Haven, but the burgers were welcomed and eagerly consumed.

As it turned out, that scheduled three-week project was completed one week early. I'm sure the frigid weather motivated the workers to step up their work pace, but I would like to think that their morale, boosted by warm hamburgers on a very cold night, helped to motivate them as well. From that time until he passed away in 1999, Jim Broman, who headed that crew, became one of my best friends.

It was always interesting to see how the cold weather in Minnesota kept presenting opportunities to demonstrate special kindnesses to telephone company employees. For instance, there was another severe snowstorm in Duluth, blocking most of the roads in and out of town. Phone and power lines were down all over the city.

Desperately trying to restore phone communications as quickly as possible, my crews worked through the evening and well into the night. It was the normal procedure to bring something for them to eat at their work site, but I felt this particular crisis called for something special, far beyond the usual. The men were doing first-class work under extremely adverse circumstances, and I wanted them to know their diligence was not going unnoticed.

I called the best nearby restaurant and order twenty filet mignon dinners to go, complete with side orders and dessert. It was an unusual order, especially since it was "to go," but the restaurant promptly complied. When I delivered the steaks, the only thing that warded off the men's shock at seeing the feast being provided was the ravenous hunger they had worked up by their frantic efforts to restore phone service. In fact, they were so excited after devouring their dinner, I believe they would have worked another two days straight if I had asked them.

A basic truth is that sheep reproduce sheep, not the shepherd. During the years I tended to my sheep, I cared for them but never produced one. Yet the shepherd has a vital, indispensable influence on the flock. As we noted earlier, we readily single out the villains of history as examples of bad leaders. And we should. But we should not underestimate the disastrous impact of "normal people" who fail to recognize or acknowledge the seriousness of their role as shepherds to people around them.

This can easily happen in a work setting where an insensitive, domineering boss can destroy company morale and eventually drive away high-quality, talented, dedicated people. It can occur in a church where a pastor falls into immoral behavior and disgrace, disillusioning members of his congregation. Poor leadership has a particularly profound and long-term influence in the home, where children eagerly imitate the actions of the parents they love.

I hate to think how often I have forgotten the importance of constantly serving as a positive example to my children and now, my grandchildren. One Saturday when our oldest daughter, Janelle, was six years old, we decided to go for a leisurely drive. I had become absorbed in the lovely scenery we were passing when she tapped me on the shoulder. "Dad, aren't you going a little too fast?" Indeed I was. Going a few miles above the speed limit hardly classified me as a felon, but Janelle's innocent question reminded me of the importance of serving as a model worth emulating, even in the seemingly small details of life.

Another time our other daughter, Jolene, was sitting with us at the kitchen table. We were engaged in a family project – memorizing Bible verses. I had been reviewing a passage with son Jim when Jolene, who had just turned four, spoke up. "I want to try one," she announced. At first I didn't respond, thinking she was too young to commit a verse from the Bible to memory. But when she repeated her desire, I said, "Okay, Jolene. Let's hear your verse." She immediately recited the verse reference, 2 Corinthians 5:17, and then repeated the verse perfectly. I was amazed. What seemed most interesting was that we had not realized she was even paying attention, yet she had followed our example precisely.

It has been said that whatever a parent does in moderation, a child will do in excess. This is a sobering thought when we consider some of the unproductive things we do routinely, hoping – consciously or subconsciously – that our offspring will never duplicate them.

Looking at the positive side of a shepherd's influence, I have admired many men and women over the years, people who have taught me a lot by their actions as well as their words. Often what has stood out most prominently is their consistency and integrity. There is no better way than to lead by example.

A shepherd must be consistent in how he treats the sheep. They require regular feeding times, ready access to water and salt, proper treatment for disease and injury, shelter from the elements, and protection from predators. Don't you, as a "sheep," need much of the same and rightfully expect it from your leaders?

When our interactions with our leaders are anchored in integrity, trust grows and we find ourselves in an environment where we can flourish as people and as workers. As Tom Peters wrote in his book, *Thriving on Chaos,* his research showed that "the best, most aggressive and successful organizations were the ones that stressed integrity and trust."[3]

Even though it has become a clich□ through the years, it remains true that honesty is the best policy. If you want a flock to be at ease – in your workplace, your home, your church, or wherever you are surrounded by people ready to follow your lead – they need to be treated with consistency and integrity. If you do so, you will have a flock willing to follow you anywhere, incredibly loyal, and extremely productive.

---

[3] Tom Peters, *Thriving on Chaos,* © 1987, Harper Collins Publishers, New York, NY, page 519.

I have also come to realize, however, that even the most admirable leaders still are imperfect human beings, just as I am. As the Bible states, "There is none righteous, not even one" (Romans 3:10).

We tend to select our shepherds – the leaders we follow – by how they look, their charisma, cleverness of speech, intelligence, or skills and talents in certain areas. Even in Christian organizations and churches, I have observed, we often use the world's standards and methods to determine who should lead us. We factor in professional success, wealth, education and other status symbols that it seems a strong leader should have. In so doing, we often pattern our own leadership styles after them. But the danger is that when we shape ourselves according to imperfection, the best we can achieve is that level of imperfection.

I have realized – and had confirmed again and again – that for human "sheep," ultimately there is but one Shepherd that we can follow who is totally dependable, the only one who serves as a perfect model. Jesus Christ said, "I am the good shepherd; and I know My own, and My own know Me, even as the Father knows Me and I know the Father – and I lay down My life for the sheep" (John 10:14-15).

At our Lake Elmo home, whenever we had visitors we would show off our sheep. Almost every time, the guest would call the sheep. If he or she didn't, I would encourage them to do so. Regardless of what the guest said or what kind of call was used, the visitor could not get the attention of the sheep. After a few minutes of watching this, I would make a quick noise, not very loud. Instantly the sheep would raise their heads and look our way. As Jesus said in comparing Himself to an earthly shepherd, "...the sheep listen to his voice. He calls his own sheep by name and leads them out... and his sheep follow him because they know his voice" (John 10:3-4).

Sheep are smart enough to understand who their true shepherd is, and they respond only to him. We need that same basic wisdom. In today's world we have countless would-be shepherds for our human flock, even some within the Church, but Jesus is the only one we can trust completely with our earthly lives and our eternal souls. As he said, "If anyone wishes to come after Me, let him deny himself, and take up his cross, and follow Me" (Matthew 16:24).

THOUGHTS TO CONSIDER AND DISCUSS:

1. Can you think of any experiences that you have had with poor shepherds, people who either did not appreciate their responsibility as leaders of the "flocks" under their care, or individuals who abused their authority? What was/is your reaction to them?

2. Contrast that to "good shepherds" you have known – at work, in your community, your family, or even at school. What made them effective leaders?

3. Now consider yourself and the leadership roles that you have, in the workplace, in your home, or in your community. How would you rate yourself as a leader – especially in light of the insights presented through the sheep anecdotes in this chapter? What areas – if any – can you identify for improvement in your own leadership skills or philosophy?

Chapter Five:
EVEN IF YOU FEEL LIKE GIVING UP, DON'T!

"And seeing the multitudes, He felt compassion for them, because they were distressed and downcast like sheep without a shepherd...." – Matthew 9:36

Our veterinarian in Lake Elmo had a saying: "A sick sheep is a dead sheep." Generally he was right. Whenever a ewe or lamb seemed ill, we would try to treat it or have the vet come by and take a look, but in most cases our flock would be diminished by one within a few days.

There are two major reasons for this. First, once a sheep becomes ill, its resistance becomes very low and it recovers very slowly. If you want hardy, resilient animals, sheep are not the ones to have.

The second reason is a simple economic consideration. Once a lamb becomes diseased, it could cost several hundred dollars to nurse it back to health. Since a fair market price for a ewe ranges from fifty to one-hundred dollars, it makes little business sense to invest a lot of money in a sick sheep. With an already low profit margin in the sheep industry, sentimentality has no place – especially when you have dozens of other sheep to care for and maintain.

However, sheep will surprise you occasionally. One evening after returning home from work, I discovered an ailing ewe in the barn. She seemed more than half dead. Lying on her side, her breathing was labored and irregular. Her eyes were watering, there was foam around her mouth, and she had a bloated appearance. Her days of producing the raw material for wool sweaters had ended, I concluded.

I called the veterinarian, and he came to examine the animal. He shook his head as he looked her over. Her chances of living through the night, he said, were virtually nonexistent. Almost as an afterthought, he gave the ewe a shot of medication, reasoning that it might help and it certainly could not do any harm. The vet was honest as he left. "I'm afraid I just cost you some money for nothing."

When I awoke the next morning, the first thing that came to my mind was the ewe. From her condition the previous evening, I had no doubt she was lying dead in the barn. I decided it would be best to dispose of the body before I began the daily chores. I felt so certain of her fate that I took a shovel from the shed nearby as I left the house and walked to the field to select a spot suitable for burying the ewe. It took an hour of hard, steady work to dig the grave. When the hole was completed, I went to the barn to collect the carcass.

Nearing the barn, I could hear the persistent bleating of a sheep eager to get out to the pasture. I was shocked to find the "dead" ewe was very much alive. In fact, that morning she looked as healthy as any of the other members of my flock! In a moment or two, I recovered from my surprise and remembered

I was still holding the shovel I had used to dig the intended grave. I felt a bit sheepish myself as I quickly hid the tool behind my back, not wanting the ewe to know that I had expected anything less than a rapid, complete recovery.

Proving her return to health was no fluke, that ewe lived a full lifespan. (We usually kept our ewes about six years before we sold them.) She also bore several lambs for us over the next years, teaching me the importance of never giving up on sheep – or people.

One of a shepherd's most important responsibilities is the well-being of his sheep. He must be a practiced observer of his flock so if something goes wrong, he can recognize it and take immediate action. As the Bible says in Proverbs 27:23, "Know well the condition of your flocks, and pay attention to your herds."

A good shepherd has learned to quickly detect any significant changes among his flock – a limping ewe, a sheep not eating properly, or perhaps one that exhibits unusual restlessness. Often the problem is minor, caused by a thorn in a foot, wire wrapped around a leg, or ligaments strained by stepping into a hole. But sheep are totally helpless and fully dependent upon the shepherd's diligent care.

How do you know when a person is down and in need of special care and attention – in the workplace, or even in the home? It takes knowing the people around you, whether it's a worker who reports to you, a co-worker, a spouse or a child. Become very familiar with how they look and act when they are up, healthy and content. That way, when you notice a drastic change, you know it's time to take remedial action.

That was the value of my Monday morning walk-arounds when I was in management with the phone company. I made a point of taking the time to greet each employee at his or her workstation and just talk. I would ask how their weekend had been, how their family was doing, things like that. Frankly, at first I had initiated this practice because it seemed like a good thing to do. Little did I know the impact it would have on the employees, or how much I would learn about them during these brief, casual times of communication.

A great asset for a shepherd in spotting troubles is becoming an expert at what a problem-free sheep looks like. A normal, healthy sheep has a straight back. Its ribs do not protrude. Its wool coat is even, dense and full, without any gaps. It is active and lively, but not overly agitated. Its eyes and nose are clear, it moves easily with other members of the flock, and it eats eagerly. If any one of these characteristics is missing, it could signal a problem and the conscientious shepherd must respond immediately.

So my weekly walk-arounds served a similar purpose as I evaluated the condition of my human "flock," individually and collectively. If one's demeanor was decidedly different, an accustomed smile absent, tone of voice unusual or eye contact inconsistent, it often meant that trouble was lurking inside that was not being expressed. While I didn't want to pry into personal matters or seem nosy, I would at least ask if something was wrong or if there was some way that I could be of aid. Sometimes it helped just to know somebody cared for them; other times people would open up and confide about a problem they were struggling with. It's not that hard being an attentive shepherd.

In the opening chapter, I told you about the ewe with the difficult delivery. This illustrated my disadvantage in being a part-time shepherd. Most of our lambs had been born normally with no difficulty, many of the deliveries occurring while I was at work. Had I been more experienced in observing ewes as their time was nearing, I might have realized in advance that this particular ewe was going to need help.

Interestingly, this acquired skill at recognizing the real thing undergirds the philosophy used by the U.S. government in training people to readily identify counterfeit currency. A friend of mine, a former Army Finance Department officer, told me about the intensive drills that agents go through as they learn how to distinguish bogus bills from the authentic. I was surprised to discover, however, that probably 90 percent of their time is spent in examining real money. They examine and study the genuine article in infinite detail, reviewing intricate markings and characteristics over and over again. The key is concentrating upon the real thing. Only during the final hours of these grueling training seminars do they finally get to inspect counterfeit money. By that time, they are so familiar with bona fide currency that fakes can be spotted very quickly.

I found that this principle has application is many areas of life, including business. As a phone company supervisor, I saw the importance of keeping careful watch over my employees, not because I distrusted them, but rather because I was concerned about their personal and vocational well-being.

Each of the people I was responsible for, in my view,

was part of a team – and a hurting team member is a serious concern. From a business standpoint, many times an employee's problems detract from his or her performance and in turn, directly or indirectly, hinder the team's overall effort. Even more important, I believe employers have an obligation to extend a helping hand whenever possible to those who work for them.

As with sheep, there are a multitude of difficulties that can affect employees. It might be personal illness, marital conflicts and other family crises, or financial pressures. Problems resulting from alcohol and drug abuse can often cause chaos in the workplace. Sometimes the situation is simply a matter of a bad job fit where an employee is either ill-suited or unfulfilled in an assigned role. Problems are a given, but the sooner they can be identified and help can be provided, the greater chance there is of salvaging the employee and returning the individual – and the work team – to full productivity. As with the shepherd watching over his sheep, and the government agent scrutinizing genuine currency, the employer needs to know the workers well enough under normal conditions so that when difficulties arise, they become evident and can be dealt with appropriately.

I try to observe this principle in our home as well. I have discovered that to be an effective, supportive husband, I need to spend an ample amount of time with my wife. After years of knowing how Ardie acts when things are going well, I can usually sense when something is wrong and try to determine if there is anything I need to do to help her.

Occasionally, we hear of people who say they were

caught totally by surprise when a spouse asked for a divorce. Obviously, when people get married they don't plan to get divorced. Something happens to shatter the hopes and expectations they had on their wedding day. For the husband whose wife demands a divorce "all of a sudden," he has made a serious error: He failed to heed the advice of the proverb to "know well the condition of your flock."

The same concept applies to a father's relationship with his children. We cannot let anything – including our jobs – get in the way of spending time with our kids and getting to know them well, their strengths, interests, needs, even their fears. Without question, the work world confronts us with continual pressures. In addition, money, success and prestige beckon to us. While there is nothing intrinsically wrong with any of these, they become wrong if we pursue them at the expense of our more important and immediate responsibilities – our families and our relationship with God.

I have known men who could not believe it when they learned a son or daughter had been arrested for a crime, or had become addicted to drugs or alcohol. But when we consider how little time the average father spends with his children – mere minutes a week, according to some studies – such surprise is understandable. How can the father who does not spend much time with his children readily notice when something is wrong? Negligent shepherds – of the sheep or human variety – can easily overlook significant changes that could serve as warnings of impending disaster.

I have known many men who have spent most

of their waking hours climbing the so-called ladder of success, armed with the excuse, "I'm really doing all this for my family." Unfortunately, in too many cases the family has suffered from neglect and virtual abandonment. That is not the way of a good shepherd!

In many businesses, taking inventory is a regularly scheduled activity. I recently went to a Wal-Mart in the early afternoon and found workers throughout the store diligently counting the quantities of everything displayed on the shelves. "Inventory" is an important function of the shepherd as well. While some people may count sheep at night to lull themselves to sleep, I found it was best to count sheep during the day while fully awake. In that way, I could make sure all of my sheep were accounted for and in good condition.

You could say that sheep are the equivalent of Murphy's Law, only in long woolen outerwear: If anything can go wrong, it will. Knowing the many misfortunes that can befall his sheep is a continual concern for the shepherd. For example, sheep can wander off into another pasture and get lost. Their heads may get stuck in a fence – a very possible consequence of the grass is greener syndrome that we discussed earlier. They can become sick, injured by stumbling, or attacked by another animal.

One particularly dire situation a sheep can find itself in is a state of being "cast." Occasionally, one of our sheep would decide to take a stroll into an unfamiliar area, oblivious to potential hazards it could encounter. Especially dangerous for our sheep were depressions in the ground that were as little as one inch to as much as one foot deep. A sheep stepping into such a natural hazard could stumble, lose its balance, flip over, and find itself lying upside down – all four feet pointed toward heaven.

Unfortunately for the sheep, when it gets into such a position, usually it is unable to turn itself over. This is true of a number of breeds, including the Southdowns we had, because of their bone structure and the cushiony nature of a thick coat of wool. When the sheep fall onto their backs, the wool is matted flat against the ground. With their short legs aimed skyward and of no use in righting themselves, sheep become utterly helpless no matter how much they struggle and wiggle.

This condition is defined as being "cast," and the sheep's only hope is the prompt arrival and assistance of its shepherd. Without help, the sheep can die within a few hours – particularly in hot weather. In that unnatural position, toxic gases accumulate within the sheep that eventually cause it to suffocate.

Sometimes I would discover a sheep's flip-flopped dilemma very quickly and hurry to its aid. All that was needed to halt the crisis was a slight nudge, enough to enable the sheep to turn onto its side. Within moments it would be back on its feet, shaking its head, and then walking away as if nothing had happened. But there were a few times when too many hours had elapsed, and I would discover a sheep still lying on its back, looking restful but in fact very dead. And all just because of the lack of a timely, helpful shove.

The Bible passage at the beginning of this chapter describes Jesus Christ seeing the people as "… downcast like sheep without a shepherd." In a literal sense, He viewed them as lying belly up and helpless, desperately needing a push to get them back on their feet.

Have you ever had that belly-up, helpless feeling? You tried everything you could imagine, but nothing seemed to work? Perhaps you had reached an impasse in a difficult business situation. Or perhaps a family problem arose that seemed insurmountable. Frustrated, you were reluctant to make any decision for fear that it might be wrong. In such instances, rather than making a bad choice, it sometimes seems the wiser course simply to do nothing at all. Even King David, the former shepherd boy, wrote in Psalm 42:5-6, "Why are you cast down, O my soul?... O my God, my soul is cast down within me...." Even the mighty king of Israel could relate to that helpless, belly-up state.

I have found that even in some extremely perplexing circumstances, when I had the cast feeling of a sheep helplessly stuck on its back, all that was required was a little nudge. Perhaps a business associate can offer some helpful insight, analyzing a situation from a slightly different perspective – going outside the nine dots, as we discussed in the previous chapter – and pointing to a solution. At other times, all we need is a word of encouragement, the gentle sort of nudge that redirects our thoughts, moving them from a negative track and back onto the positive, and reenergizes us.

Now that we no longer live on a farm, and we have long since bade farewell to our flock, I no longer have to scour pastures in search of cast sheep. However, recalling the help I received at times when I became "cast," I still try to remain alert for downcast people. Sometimes I even find them in my own home.

74

When I uprooted my family from Minnesota and we moved to Chattanooga, Tennessee in the mid-1980's, the transition was relatively simple for me. I had the excitement of a new job and was working with a number of people I already knew well. This change, however, was harder for my family, particularly for Janelle, who by that time was a teenager and midway through high school. It had been difficult for her to leave old friends, favorite activities and familiar places. Ardie and I made a point of talking to her often, encouraging her to look upon our move as a positive experience. Once she made new friends her attitude changed, but it took awhile. In the meantime, she needed the assurance and comfort of our love and concern for her.

I don't succeed as much as I would like, but I work at giving my family the proper place in my life. The Bible teaches that our priorities should be God first, wife and family second, followed by vocation, hobbies and interests, etc. Yet we live in a society where so much of our identity and sense of self-worth is bound up in our work. It is a temptation, possibly even more for men than for most women, to move our jobs up to the No. 2 priority, perhaps even No. 1.

In my experience, I have found it helps to keep in mind the scriptural admonition in 1 Timothy 5:8 that says if a man does not care for his family, he is "worse than an infidel." Therefore, before I try playing good Samaritan and go looking for fallen "sheep" outside of our home, I need to make sure there are no "cast" members of the Johnson flock that need my full and immediate attention.

At work I have always felt a similar responsibility.

It's critical to recognize people as individuals with real needs and concerns, not merely as instruments for achieving goals and objectives. In American business circles, we often say our most valuable resource is people, but the tendency is to pay more attention to our machines and tools than we do to our employees. The problem is, machines don't become cast – but people do!

Countless times I have observed in the business world how important this realization can be. Employees who are healthy physically, mentally and emotionally are far more productive in their work. At the same time, they usually respond with their best efforts when they know their leader has a sincere interest in their welfare. Management by manipulation or intimidation may succeed over the short term, but its long-term impact can be devastating, demoralizing, even disastrous for a company and its people.

My children all are adults and married now, but I will always remember the times when I started to forget my responsibilities as a shepherd both at home and at work. The kids had a knack for reminding me. During our years in Lake Elmo, it amazed me to discover how much better the children knew our sheep than I did. Jim or Janelle would point to a ewe and announce, "Hey, Dad, I think that one is going to have a lamb next." I would reply, "Oh, yeah?" conceding that most of the time I could not tell – and didn't know how they could. The kids usually were very accurate. Being the "shepherd," that was a humbling admission for me, but a wonderful reminder: "Johnson," I would think to myself, "you're not as good an observer as you think you are."

Earlier I mentioned about Janelle's struggle when we relocated from Minnesota to Chattanooga. When we moved back to Minnesota, her sister experienced a similar problem. Chattanooga was virtually all that Jolene had known, since we had lived there for 10 years. The separation from dear friends and favorite activities threw her into a downward spiral. Recognizing her depressed state, we seriously discussed moving back to Chattanooga since at that point geographic location was not critical for the work I was doing. We even let her fly back to Chattanooga on her own and stay with friends for a while, planning for her to enroll in school there. Slowly, she warmed to the idea of going back to her native state. Our willingness to work with her, being sensitive to her needs, was a key part of this transition.

What about the "flocks" for which you are responsible, whether in your home, where you work, or even through community activities? Have you been watching the sheep as diligently as you should? I learned that you never know when you will come across a cast sheep. Prompt attention can make a world of difference. As they say, prevention is always preferable to the cure.

THOUGHTS TO CONSIDER AND DISCUSS:

1. When the going gets tough, the tough get going, they say. But often it's easier to give up. Can you think of an instance when you gave up when confronted by a seemingly insurmountable problem, but later wished that you had tried harder and stayed with it longer? What about a different time, an instance when you did persevere and were glad that you had?

2. How would you go about recognizing a "sick lamb" or "cast sheep" in your own sphere of influence – at home, on the job, at your church or an organization where you are actively involved? Read the advice in 1 Peter 5:2-3.

3. In your family or business, can you think of any "counterfeits" you are accepting at the expense of the authentic? How does the exhortation in Philippians 4:8 apply to such situations?

Chapter Six:
DON'T LET THEM PULL
THE WOOL OVER YOUR EYES

"Then I will give you shepherds after My own heart, who will feed you on knowledge and understanding." – Jeremiah 3:15

Have you ever wondered where the old saying, "Don't let them pull the wool over your eyes," came from? Like the "grass is greener," and perhaps a few of our other familiar adages, I believe it started with an observant, practical-minded shepherd.

All sheep grow wool, but not all sheep grow wool equally. Most of the time on our farm we raised a breed of sheep called Suffolk. The short-haired, black muzzles of the Suffolks made for a striking contrast to their cream-colored coats of wool, particularly just before shearing time (which we will discuss in chapter 9).

However, another type of sheep we had for awhile, called Southdown, grew wool everywhere, even over its face. This distinctive breed literally would have the wool pulled over its eyes by the natural process of growth. To remedy this problem, we would have to trim the wool from their faces regularly. Otherwise, the plentiful wool would droop over their foreheads and around their eyes, hindering their sight. I suppose it would be like trying to walk with a thick wool sweater over your head. Unless we responded promptly with the clippers, these sheep would have difficulty just seeing where they were going or finding food.

The warning about having wool pulled over one's eyes may have been code language among shepherds to remind one another to guard against dishonest transactions with other people. By observing their sheep, these diligent men of the cloth – woolen cloth, that is – had learned well the perils of obscured vision.

Generally, the problem of wool over the eyes for human sheep is far more subtle. It can result from intended deception, or be the product of our own lack of awareness. In my fifty-plus years of driving automobiles, few things have been more frustrating than trying to maneuver through thick fog. You don't know what lies ahead, and you aren't sure what may be approaching from behind.

We can experience the same effect when we are evaluating and weighing an important decision. The way might seem clouded as we search for the right path, and we can empathize with the poor Southdown sheep whose negligent shepherd has forgotten to cut away the bothersome wool.

One reason we often have trouble dealing with circumstances present and future is our difficulty in viewing them objectively and honestly. This type of blindness can be as disabling as that suffered by the wooly-eyed Southdown. It could be that we are truly helpless in being able to remove this "wool." What can we do to overcome such a dilemma?

For me, the answer is found in the form of personal accountability to another individual or a small group of men. A person that I trust and who knows me well – much like the relationship between sheep and their shepherd – can be very helpful in pointing out problems and blind spots, which often are surprisingly obvious to someone else.

This principle first became evident to me when I became involved with a group of Christian businessmen in 1970. One of the immediate benefits for me was being able to meet other Christian businessmen and discuss common concerns and interests with them. As I developed close friendships with some of the men, we began to build accountability into our relationships. We would openly discuss problems and needs, offering encouragement, but we also felt the freedom to challenge one another if we felt someone had gotten off track in a particular area.

Like the times when we would trim the obstructing wool from around the eyes of our sheep, we would help one another to put biblical principles into action, pointing out any instances in which we might not be seeing clearly. At times we would admonish one another boldly, using God's Word as our source of authority, whether the problem concerned our spiritual growth, business practices or family relationships.

I'm convinced that one reason many people are struggling in their lives today is that they have no one to remove the wool from their eyes. They are not accountable to anyone, so there is no one to help them see their shortcomings or other critical areas that need attention.

It was in the context of accountability that I arrived at my decision to leave my career at the telephone company in 1971. Once a week I would meet with a group of businessmen for prayer and Bible study. One of the men I met there was Chuck McKenzie, the president and owner of a small service company. He desired to become more involved in faith-based enterprises, but the business was consuming him, his time and energy. Chuck understood the reality that his business was his ministry, and his ministry was his business, but he had a unique opportunity to go to Africa for a year, serving as an engineer and assisting in getting a power plant back on line. He was eager to respond and meet a critical need for missionaries there, but he could not just abandon his company.

While we were discussing this, I offhandedly suggested, "Why don't you get more involved, and I'll run the business for you?" I had said that in jest. I had enjoyed my years at the phone company and knew very little about Chuck's business, which involved the remanufacture of acetylene-oxygen welding equipment and medical regulators used in hospitals. Chuck didn't realize that I was joking, however, and surprised me by accepting my offer.

Six weeks later, after prayer and much deliberation, I found myself making a major job transition. Suddenly, instead of supervising a crew of approximately one hundred people, maintaining telephone service for St. Paul and adjacent suburbs, I was learning how to run a company of just twenty employees. It was a traumatic change for awhile. At first I didn't even have a desk of my own, but the move proved to be a good one. Over time I found the challenge of running a different kind of business to be greatly stimulating, and both Chuck and I were able to devote more time to activities and projects directly related to advancing the cause of Christ.

Wool covering the eyes was not the only annoyance for my sheep. Ticks, small parasites that would bore through the wool and into the sheep's bodies, were another nagging problem. The ticks could reproduce quickly and, before long, the entire flock would become infested.

Hosting a heavy population of ticks can be debilitating for a sheep. It becomes run down physically, and the quality of its wool diminishes as a result. Because of their thick wool, our sheep often had to be in a state of obviously declining health before we would become aware of the ticks and begin taking steps to combat them.

Today, years later, ticks can be eliminated fairly easily by spraying the sheep with newly developed insecticides. But when we were raising our sheep, it was not as simple. We had to dip our sheep in a special solution, putting them into a tank we converted from a 55-gallon drum. The greatest difficulty was getting the sheep to cooperate. They particularly disliked having their heads dunked into the liquid, but it was necessary to kill the ticks and put our animals on recovery road.

As a shepherd, I knew the experience was not pleasant for the sheep. It may even have been frightening for them to suddenly become submerged into a chemical solution. But having no way to explain our intentions, we just forced the animals to comply.

With the sheep, the troubling ticks were literally

closer than skin, since they would burrow beneath the skin's surface. In spite of that, the sheep appeared unaware of their plight. It took an outsider – their shepherd – to notice something was wrong, and then prescribe and implement procedures to rectify the problem. Even if our sheep had understood their situation, they would not have known what to do about it.

In business we sometimes undertake programs that serve as the equivalent of dipping the sheep. We may call in consultants (if you have been in the work world for a long time, you may remember when we called them "efficiency experts") to observe and determine whether there are any "ticks" in our systems and operational practices. Sometimes, even though we know their recommendations are for our ultimate good, we strongly resist any corrective measures because of immediate uncertainties.

I have known many businessmen who displayed a tendency to "wing it," taking the attitude that, "It's my company, and I'm going to run it my way!" Frequently, that frame of mind can prove self-destructive. Entrepreneurs like this may have excellent products or services to offer, but due to a lack of good advice – or their unwillingness to heed counsel that is given – their businesses can falter, even fail.

This is one reason it is so important for any business or organization to have a board of advisors, concerned about the company and its leadership, but not intimately tied to it. Proverbs 11:14 and Proverbs 15:22 teach us about the wisdom gained from a number of trusted counselors. These are the people who can spot the "ticks" afflicting us even when we are oblivious to them.

There is a need to be wary, however, of pitfalls inherent to selecting a board of directors. It's important that the members are not "yes men," a group that simply rubber-stamps whatever the leader intends to do. They need to be strong, independent thinkers who care enough for the organization to speak up and take action if they sense something may be out of line. With some non-profit boards I have worked with, members have been appointed to rotating terms, serving for several years and then being replaced. While this does provide for a continual supply of fresh insights, it also can mean that by the time the directors fully understand the organization and recognize the need for changes, their terms are up.

Too often we make a mistake in thinking we have to be accountable to no one. As followers of Christ, we are commanded ultimately to be accountable to God, and if we desire for our plans to succeed and our lives to stay on the right track, it also helps to be accountable to others who have a sincere, objective concern for us and our well-being.

This awareness served as the impetus for starting Christian Network Teams in the early 1990's. As I met with CEOs and business owners, it became clear that many of them needed a group of advisors who could assist them not only in good business practices, but also in discerning how to apply biblical principles to various issues and needs. They have found a place where they can be transparent and accountable to a team of men they can trust, individuals who genuinely are looking out for their best interests. In a sense, it's like having Christ-centered board of directors, people who know how to dig into the Scriptures to find answers to pressing problems.

Of course, you don't have to be a businessperson to find value in this accountability concept. It works in the home, and other settings, as well. Sometimes a family problem may persist, seemingly defying solution. It may be that we are too close to the situation and thereby unable to properly evaluate all of the factors involved or possible remedies. The help of a trained, certified family counselor may be necessary, but not always. I have often found the insights of good friends can work wonders in bringing a fresh perspective to a stressful situation.

We all have heard the phrase, "Tell it like it is." This is exactly what we need at times, even though it may hurt or cause us to feel uncomfortable. The book of Proverbs frequently reminds us that, even though counsel may not always seem pleasant, a wise man becomes wiser when he heeds the advice of credible observers.

My sheep taught me a third lesson in mutual cooperation, although this last one came more indirectly. From time to time it became necessary to erect temporary gates while we were mending a fence or to guide the sheep into another section of pasture. Since we usually needed the new gates for only a short time, sometimes for just a few hours, we would use twine instead of wire to fasten them.

The twine was very strong, used originally to tie up a tarpaulin or to secure hay bales. The secret to the twine's strength was that it consisted of as many as twenty separate but intertwined strands. Ecclesiastes 4:12 observes, "a cord of three strands is not quickly torn apart." Since our twine had many more than three strands, we never worried about whether it would hold a temporary gate in its place.

This strength did present one minor disadvantage: The twine was far too strong to break with our hands, no matter how we strained and tugged, yet sometimes we were too far from the house to get a knife or scissors if we had forgotten to bring them with us. Our solution to this dilemma was to painstakingly separate individual strands of the twine and break them one at a time. Working together, the braids were extremely strong, but individually, they were relatively weak. By popping the strands one by one, the twine could be pulled apart.

In a sense, each strand of the twine was accountable to the others. They supported and gave strength to one another and worked together in a classic example of successful teamwork. Only when we separated these "team members" did they become ineffective and easily broken.

Have you ever seen this principle in action in the workplace? Sometimes we will find a very talented employee who insists on functioning as a "lone ranger," doing his or her job apart from the company team. Such a person can be very productive, but there is always a danger that the employee may prove to be a disruptive factor in any efforts designed to get people working together more smoothly.

Another instance would be a working environment in which morale is low; there is no effort to encourage a sense of teamwork and harmony, and employees find themselves working independently – sometimes leading to conflict. Such conditions could be a result of management policies, or because the leadership has not been alert to identify such a problem. The future for such an organization can be ominous. Once the individual employee "strands" start to break, the strength of the company "twine" begins to decrease substantially.

A much more encouraging scenario is a situation where the employees have a good understanding of each other's roles in the company, respect one another's talents and contributions, and can see how their respective jobs fit together to accomplish a common goal. In this type of environment, productivity and job satisfaction are usually high, and prospects for the business's bottom line at the end of the year are very good.

On our farm, whenever we had to erect a new fence for our sheep, we could readily observe the importance of teamwork. I learned that fence construction is a virtual art form. The fence posts not only determine a fence line and hold up the woven wire, but also work together to support the barrier. Individual posts are not strong enough to withstand the weight and stresses of a tightly strung fence, so diagonal wires must be strung – crossing each other – so the pressure becomes distributed more evenly from post to post. Once a horizontal beam is fixed between the posts to keep them from sagging together, the diagonal wires are put into place. The final step is to secure the woven wire fencing into the posts, stretching it as tightly as possible, and then fastening it.

These separate elements of the fence combine to form one functioning unit to achieve a singular purpose. The whole does in fact become greater than the sum of the parts. In my case, fence construction became far more than just learning abstract principles about teamwork. It even helped Ardie and me strengthen the foundation of our marriage.

Erecting a fence, as you can imagine, is definitely not a job for one individual. At our "Johnson Acres," it often became a one-man/one-woman project. My wife and I spent countless hours together building and repairing fences over the years. We have since concluded that the team sense we gained from working together to get those jobs completed contributed substantially to where we are in our marriage today.

I'm not suggesting that the remedy for a troubled marriage—or a struggling business—is to go out and start putting up sheep fences. But in a marital relationship, if couples spent more time together, working toward mutually desired goals, I'm convinced there would be healthier marriages and far fewer divorces. Too few couples are pulling together to build anything of value; they are occupied with doing their own thing and, consequently, wind up being pulled apart.

From the day we exchanged wedding vows, Ardie and I viewed ourselves as partners in a lifetime venture. We have endeavored to co-labor on each aspect of our marriage and family as a team, whether it involved raising the children, handling our finances, making career decisions, serving in our church, entertaining guests, or determining where to spend our vacations.

For more than 40 years, like those strands of twine and the fence posts working in mutual cooperation, we have supported one another and been mutually accountable. We have experienced the truth of Ecclesiastes 4:9, which says, "Two are better than one because they have a good return for their labor."

As a businessman, my association with other followers of Christ in business has provided a similar benefit. I have received encouragement to strive to put biblical principles into practice on the job. In addition, I have often been reminded of the importance of sharing my faith in Jesus with others whenever opportunities arose. I understood that my primary purpose on the job was to serve and represent my Lord, enabling others to see His importance in my life and to realize what He could mean for their lives as well.

Even after leaving what we typically term the "secular" business world (a distinction we never see in the Bible) to engage in full-time vocational ministry with business and professional people, the importance of being held accountable remained as great. I have continued to meet monthly with a small group of men to study the Bible and maintain financial and spiritual accountability with one another. This has been extremely helpful in keeping me focused on those things in life that are truly important and enduring.

Dr. Howard Hendricks, a popular speaker, author, and member of the Dallas Theological Seminary faculty, attests to the importance of personal accountability. Several times I have heard him state that even after many years of ministry and Christian leadership roles, his spiritual growth and ministry effectiveness have been measurably enhanced by continuing to be an active participant in an accountability group.

Sheep differ sharply from people in that they cannot be held personally accountable, but that underscores their reliance on the shepherd. Their well-being rests entirely on the accountability and diligence of the shepherd in fulfilling his responsibilities to them. From a Christian standpoint, we ultimately must recognize that we are accountable to God. Our Shepherd, Jesus Christ, made many promises to us that are recorded in the Scriptures. Because of His nature, He voluntarily became accountable to us for their fulfillment.

The most exciting aspect of this relationship is that, unlike human accountability partners, the Lord's vision and discernment is not limited or obstructed. He sees clearly – straight to the heart. "For God sees not as man sees, for man looks at the outward appearance, but the Lord looks at the heart" (1 Samuel 16:7). Another passage, Proverbs 21:2, says, "Every man's way is right in his own eyes, but the Lord weighs the hearts."

Interestingly, although I know this and believe it, for some reason it often seems easier to be accountable to another person – someone I can see and touch. It is, therefore, extremely important to make sure that person is committed to Christ and will remain faithful to the Word of God as he responds to me and affirms my accountability.

Let me suggest, just for a moment, that you ask yourself a few questions: To whom are you accountable? Who is close enough to you to check for troublesome "ticks," or is concerned enough about you to ensure that "wool" does not grow over your eyes, obscuring your sight as you proceed through life? Do you have at least one person working in tandem with you to assist in achieving a common goal? Or are you like a fragile ball of string, consisting of a single strand, hoping desperately not to snap under great pressure?

THOUGHTS TO CONSIDER AND DISCUSS:

1. All of us have found ourselves caught with the "wool over our eyes" at one time or another. What was one example of this that you can recall in your own life?

2. Do you have someone who cares enough to remove the wool from your eyes, if and when it occurs? If so, describe this relationship. If not, what steps could you take to establish a helpful accountability relationship with another individual?

3. Does the thought of relying on another person for strength, support or accountability seem threatening or make you feel uncomfortable? Why or why not? (See Galatians 6:1-2 for another perspective on this.)

Chapter Seven:
IT'S HARD TO KICK WHEN YOU'RE ON YOUR KNEES

"He flees because he is a hireling, and is not concerned about the sheep." – John 10:13

Sometimes the helplessness of a sheep extends to the relatively simple task of eating. Lambs, like human babies, almost immediately upon being born begin searching for something to eat. A lamb, after recovering from the shock of leaving the cozy, warm womb of the ewe to enter the world, instinctively knows the best food source is its mother. In most cases the lamb easily locates the milk supply, but occasionally its desire can be thwarted by something as innocuous as a clump of wool.

If the ewe has not been trimmed prior to the birth, wool may obstruct the lamb's access to the mother's milk. The hungry newborn, anxious to eat but not certain what it is looking for, may clamp onto the wool, presuming that to be the food source. The baby sheep is not particularly selective, and the wool is in the general vicinity of where instinct tells the newborn to go. If you have ever removed a woolen mitten by grabbing it in your teeth and pulling, you can empathize with the lamb's dilemma. It's not very nutritional, and you can't say much for the taste either, but if not given assistance, the lamb may persist with the mouthful of wool, thinking food must be in there somewhere.

I usually tried to head off this problem by inspecting the expectant ewe in advance and clipping away any excess wool that could frustrate the hungry newborn. Actually, I never received any thanks for my concern and attentiveness, but part of a shepherd's job is serving as an unsung hero.

In rare instances, a lamb would arrive a bit short in the instinct department. The confused little sheep would seem unable to grasp the relationship between his eager mouth and mom's milk glands. That can be a problem, since the first few hours are critical to a lamb's development.

At those times I would take the logical course of action, getting on my knees to provide personalized assistance and direction for the lamb. Kneeling down beside the ewe, I would guide the lamb to its mother's milk. The task simply required taking the little head, directing it under the ewe and connecting its mouth to the "spigot." But the simplicity of this task did not minimize its importance. There was something humbling about kneeling to assist a tiny lamb in performing a natural function, but it also was rewarding to know I could provide such an essential service.

There also were a few occasions when the feeding problem was not of the lamb's doing. A ewe might prove to be a balky, unresponsive parent. The lamb would be urgently trying to grab hold of the milk sack, but the ewe would refuse to stand still. This could be due to maternal indifference; the ewe might prefer to concentrate on eating than on feeding; or she might be tender, making the lamb's sucking painful for her.

Again, in these situations the observant shepherd must spring into action. The most practical solution is to turn the ewe into a cast sheep, immobilizing her on her back. I would never leave a mother in that position for long, but it would give the lamb an opportunity to eat without having to chase a moving target.

As a manager in business, there were times when I had to take similar action. For instance, a new employee might need some personalized coaxing (or coaching) to get off to a good start. Some employers believe in an "ivory tower" approach to management, where instructions are passed along to staff people only at an arm's length distance. This, however, was never my philosophy. I would not do the employee's work for him, but neither did I see it as a matter of sink or swim.

I have often heard it said that the best leader is one who will never ask anyone to do something he would not be willing to do himself or herself. I agree, because this means at times the boss will need to come alongside employees – perhaps getting down on the knees if necessary – to help, whether it involves providing necessary training or helping in the completion of an important job.

Another benefit of at least occasional close interaction with workers is being able to fully understand what is expected of them. At the same time, I often found that as a manager I was able to gain a much better understanding from them of what it took to get a certain job or project completed.

In this respect, I have found job descriptions to be extremely helpful, not only in the workplace but also in the home, at church, and even with volunteer organizations. People like to know what is expected of them.

Years ago I heard a conference speaker recount a major dilemma in his company that came about because of an unclear job description. An employee had been with the company for several months, but he was just not working out. It seemed evident that the man could not do his job, so he would have to be dismissed.

This employee was called into his boss's office. The manager felt badly about having to terminate this very likeable individual, so he decided to ease into the matter, hoping that they could both recognize the problem and the need for corrective measures.

"How are things going for you on the job?" the manager asked. The employee's eyes brightened and he quickly responded, "Great!"

"Really?" the boss asked.

"Oh, yes, just terrific!" the worker replied with great enthusiasm.

Somewhat puzzled, the manager suggested, "Well, uh, tell me exactly what you're doing." The employee proceeded to detail the many jobs he was doing, and in fact, he was doing those very well. The problem was that they did not represent the job he had been hired to perform. Soon it became evident to the manager that the difficulty was not one of unsatisfactory performance, but rather a case of unclear and misunderstood expectations. The employee had never received a definitive job description; it was merely presumed that he knew what he was supposed to do. Obviously a dangerous assumption!

When the meeting concluded, the employee was not dismissed. In fact, he received a pay increase – based on the quality of the work he had done, even though it had not been the work his superiors had expected him to carry out. The worker also was given a very clear, specific job description so there would be no more confusion about what he was supposed to be doing.

Thinking about this story, it reminded me of a newborn lamb struggling to find its first meal. Like the lamb, the employee had been willing to do whatever was required, but needed help in locating the target.

One of the factors in my decision in the late 1970's to take on a full-time staff role in ministry with business and professional men was the approach taken by the man who interviewed me. Actually, at the time it had not even felt like I was being interviewed. One day Max called and asked if he could meet with Ardie and me to discuss our openness to taking a position with an organization I had been involved with as a volunteer, Christian Business Men's Committee. I explained to Max that we already had plans for our annual family excursion to the cabin we had in northern Minnesota. He asked if he and his wife, Mildred, could come up to visit with us. I told him that would be fine. I knew it would involve a long drive from their home in Kansas City, Missouri, but nevertheless, they arrived as promised.

We thoroughly enjoyed their visit. What impressed me most was the complete lack of formality during our time together, and Max's sincere interest in me as a person, not just as a prospective employee. At no time did I ever feel like I was "under inspection." Their concern was not only for me, but also for Ardie and our children. We did discuss what my responsibilities would be in the role I was considering, but it was Max's low-key approach and genuine interest that convinced me that it would be enjoyable to work for him.

Job descriptions can be helpful in the home environment as well. Borrowing an idea from my friend, Dr. Henry Brandt, and his late wife, Eva, through the years I occasionally referred to myself as the president of the Johnson Family Corporation and Ardie as the vice president in charge of the home. We don't have a formal contract stipulating this, but we do operate with this as a guiding philosophy.

Especially as our children were growing up, my attitude was that since Ardie was spending much more time in our home and with our children than I did, she had a much better idea of what was needed in those areas. She frequently would discuss a problem with me, but I noticed that things ran much more smoothly when I delegated to her both the responsibility and authority for everyday household operations and decisions.

Another aspect of a shepherd's "on the knees" relationship to his sheep is described in John 10:12-13:

He who is a hireling, and not a shepherd, who is not the owner of the sheep, beholds the wolf coming, and leaves the sheep, and flees, and the wolf snatches them and scatters them. He flees because he is a hireling, and is not concerned about the sheep.

The difference between the hireling and the shepherd primarily is one of commitment. A shepherd who establishes a close, compassionate and caring link with his sheep is ready to respond in whatever ways necessary to ensure the welfare of the flock. This might range from helping the ewe and lamb come together initially for feeding time to protecting the animals from wolves and other predators.

The hireling, however, is simply that. He has been hired to perform a specific job and sees no need to do anything additional. He has no moral or legal commitment to the flock, and lacks the loyal attachment of the shepherd. For instance, instead of getting down to guide the lamb to its mother's milk, the hireling would be more likely to kick the lamb toward the ewe, if he bothers to do anything at all. Basically, his attitude is that if the lamb manages to figure out what it should do to eat, fine. If not, too bad. There will be other lambs.

In this or any scenario, the hireling is not the person you want to rely on in a crisis. The hireling's motto is most likely to be, "When the going gets tough, it's time to get going – as fast and as far away as possible!"

Even if someone has never read the 10th chapter of the Gospel of John before, its meaning can be readily understood. Parents usually search long and carefully before selecting a babysitter, especially if their children are very young or they expect to be gone for an extended period of time. If a problem arises, they want someone who will respond quickly and responsibly, not someone who will panic at the onset of trouble.

And children, from the time they are born, grasp the shepherd/lamb relationship even if they can't articulate it. Usually, they rely completely on mom and dad, trusting that they will always be there to meet their needs and provide timely assistance. Whether this means changing a diaper, pitching in with the homework, or lending a sympathetic ear and shoulder following the breakup of a young romance, children rightfully expect their parents to be "on call" twenty-four hours a day.

In today's society, however, the predominant attitude seems to be more like that of the hireling. "Commitment, what's that?" is the attitude reflected by the words and deeds of many people we know. Tragically, this commodity is glaringly absent in many marriages, job settings, and even in friendships. I suppose this is why so many people today relate to the mantra of "It's all about you," or "Look out for yourself, because that's all that you've got." They realize how rare it is to find people you can truly depend on, so the best course of action, they reason, is to put all of your trust in yourself.

One of my great joys as a follower of Christ is knowing that I don't have to rely solely on myself. I do have the responsibility to do the best I can, but after having let others – and myself – down many, many times, I need someone who is more trustworthy and dependable than I am.

I suppose it's natural that we feel the greatest need to pray when things are not going well. We may be kicking and screaming about our circumstances, but when we approach God in prayer, something supernatural occurs. Whenever I get on my knees to talk to God, it does something for my perspective regardless of what problems may be weighing on my mind. Perhaps then, more than ever, I am reminded that I am one of His sheep and I need to again place my complete trust in Him, just as my sheep put their unquestioning confidence in me. There is a saying that I believe speaks volumes, regardless of whether you have experienced being a shepherd: "It's hard to kick when you're on your knees."

When Ardie was a young girl on the farm, she spent much of her time in the fields watching over the sheep – particularly the young lambs. While she was near them, the observant sheep generally were calm, and there were no incidents. However, often while she was away from the sheep, wolves would sneak up and attack. The problem became so severe that Ardie's parents eventually stopped raising sheep and, instead, began working with cattle because they were much better equipped to ward off wolves. During their last year in the sheep business, her family saw more than 100 lambs in their flock killed by wolves.

For sheep, age and experience are matters of minor consequence. They didn't worry that Ardie was a girl. All they knew was that when she was on duty as the shepherd, the flock enjoyed peace and safety. When she was gone, their danger was continual and they remained in a state of constant anxiety. Relating that to our own circumstances, we know that the omnipresent, all-knowing God, our Shepherd, has promised, "I will never desert you, nor will I ever forsake you" (Hebrews 13:5). This should give us the great assurance that even when times and events seem most discouraging, God is with us. He stands ever ready to give whatever help we need and to defend us against any and all enemies.

Many times I witnessed how a lamb, seeing the

shepherd on his knees to offer assistance, seemed to relax, contented and reassured that he was in capable hands. I have found the converse to be true in our relationship with God. When we spend time on our knees, talking and listening to Him, we become able to let go of the anxieties of the day that have weighed us down.

Recently I was meditating on Philippians 4:7, in which we find the promise of "...the peace of God, which surpasses all comprehension...." As I pondered this verse, I realized that the promise is conditional upon our observing the command of the passage that immediately precedes it. That verse instructs us not to be anxious, but, "...in everything by prayer and supplication with thanksgiving," to present our requests to God. I have found that if I spend consistent time with my Shepherd and get to know Him intimately, I have absolute trust in His promise to guide me through all of life's anxious and trying moments.

If we ignore His presence, or do not give ourselves the opportunity to see Him at work in our lives, we can understandably expect to feel distress and despair when our life's road gets rough.

There was another time when my son, Jim, taught me a simple but important lesson in prayer. The situation was not nearly as dire as when the ewe was struggling in labor, but it did provide another illustration of how God honors childlike faith – whether it is exhibited by a child, or an adult.

One summer I was laboring with our church softball team. I use the term "laboring" because that is what I was doing; I was not *playing* softball. Softball had never been my best sport, and throughout the season my best hit had never advanced me beyond first base. One night, Jim and I knelt by his bed as he said his prayers. To my surprise, he asked, "and please, God, help my Dad get past first base." I was surprised. Jim was our team's bat boy and he had observed my "single-mindedness" on the softball field.

So as I took the field for the next game, I could not stop thinking about how trustingly my son had prayed for improvement in his father's batting prowess.

During the game I came to the plate several times, but if you had judged by my performance alone, there would have been no indication that the object was to advance beyond first base. On my final time at home plate, I looked out of the corner of my eye toward the stands and saw my son watching intently. "Lord," I prayed, "I sure don't want to disappoint Jim." (Later, I would learn that Jim had continued to pray fervently as well: "Dear God, please help my Dad get at least to second base.")

To my surprise – and probably to everyone else's as well – I made solid contact with the ball and it soared majestically into the outfield. Although I hadn't done it all season, I rounded first base as gracefully as I could – as if it was something I did all of the time – and steamed into second base. I had a double! Not only that, but my hit also drove in our team's winning run. The team, as excited as we were about the big hit, called it the "holy double."

To this day, I have never been approached by a representative of the softball hall of fame to recount the mighty blow I struck to propel our team to victory. But that day I was a hero to one little boy who saw his simple, trusting prayers answered.

There is much that we can learn on our knees, whether it is showing a lamb the way to its personal dairy, assisting an associate at work, encouraging a family member, or best of all, enjoying the fellowship of our loving, faithful God.

THOUGHTS TO CONSIDER AND DISCUSS:

1. Try to think of someone who was concerned enough to come alongside of you – perhaps even on his or her knees – and offer help. Who was it, and what kind of help was offered? How would you relate Proverbs 18:24 to this experience?

2. Patience, it is said, is a virtue. How can you build – and demonstrate – a greater degree of patience with family members, business associates and friends? How – if at all – could you see the principles stated in Hebrews 10:36 and James 1:3-4 applying here?

3. Have you ever responded to a situation as a "hireling," fleeing when adversity presented itself? How would you assess your level of commitment to your friends, your job and work associates, your family, or other personal activities or responsibilities?

Chapter Eight:
HOW MUCH IS TOO MUCH?

"I will feed them in a good pasture, and their
grazing ground will be the mountain heights of
Israel." – Ezekiel 34:14

Once upon a pasture
There stood a lonely ewe;
Her stomach was looking bloated,
She was feeling really blue.

She'd eaten some alfalfa,
She'd consumed some clover, too;
'Twas too late she realized, she'd
Eaten more than she should chew.

– R.T.

When was the last time you gorged yourself on a good meal? Thanksgiving Day? Christmas? Or maybe the last time you went to that buffet restaurant that serves twenty-five different salads and vegetables, seven kinds of meat, five varieties of rolls and breads, and sixteen types of dessert? Can you remember someone telling you, "If I eat one more bite, I think I'll burst"?

We all enjoy indulging in delicious meals, but

sometimes there is a price to be paid afterward – and I'm not referring to the restaurant bill. You may recall a TV commercial years ago that featured an obviously uncomfortable man seated at a dinner table who kept repeating, "I can't believe I ate the whole thing!" In the background could be heard the harsh voice of his unsympathetic wife assuring him, "You ate it, Ralph!"

Gluttony seems to be one of mankind's favorite sins, but people are not the only ones to suffer from such maladies. Sheep can be equally guilty of overeating, especially when they are let loose to graze in some lush pasture. For them, the consequences can be disastrous, far more troublesome than the need to grab an antacid tablet or two. We humans have heard that, "You can get too much of a good thing," and also that, "It's not good to do anything to excess." Sheep, however, either have never heard such warnings or simply choose not to pay any attention to them.

Legumes such as leafy alfalfa and clover, very attractive to a sheep's eye, can devastate a flock. These plants, pleasing to a sheep's palate, can cause a rapid accumulation of stomach gases. Some varieties of alfalfa actually cause a froth or foamy material to form in the abdominal cavity, preventing the necessary elimination of these gases. This bloating effect can cause the sheep's left side to bulge abnormally and force rapid, shallow respiration. Such a condition, if not promptly treated, can result in more than simple discomfort. In extreme cases, the sheep's stomach can become paralyzed, leading to death within a few hours.

Again it falls to the shepherd to remain alert so

he can recognize this potential hazard for his flock. If he spots a pasture that could seem so inviting that his sheep could unwittingly start eating themselves to death, he can take precautionary measures by first feeding them dry hay. This coarse feed helps to stimulate a sheep's belching mechanism and keeps the ingested greens from forming into a health-threatening mass in the stomach.

In the event that a sheep does become bloated, there are various preparations available for treating the ailment. There also are time-honored remedies, ranging from massaging the animal's abdomen to the extreme of having a veterinarian puncture the stomach to permit the gases and froth to escape (only for emergencies).

You might be thinking that you now know more about a sheep's digestive process than you ever cared to know, but I offer it only because the principle applies to human sheep as well. I may never have eaten so much that I needed to have my stomach punctured, but I have overdone myself in other areas of life. We all can recall times when we have done things like expose ourselves to too much sun, overwork, exercise to excess, waste too much time, or spend far too much money on a shopping trip. When sheep become bloated, the problem can usually be traced to their diet. People, however, seem to have a knack for becoming bloated on a variety of things.

You might be surprised to know that in my opinion, it's possible to become spiritually bloated – even for devoted followers of Jesus Christ. Now, more than at any other time in history, we have the advantage of indulging in a bountiful smorgasbord of Christian teaching. We have many thousands of books, periodicals, tapes, CDs and DVDs on all areas of Christian living. We also have ready access to a multitude web sites, films, seminars, conferences, retreats, TV shows (and networks), toys, games and crafts, all of which claim to be able to draw us closer to God. And this does not even count the variety of activities we can take part in through our local congregations.

Ironically, despite such unprecedented abundance of spiritual resources, studies consistently report that the impact of the gospel on our society appears to be comparatively minor. We could point to the shift of the majority of society toward a godless, secularized worldview. But how can we explain that although as many as half of the people surveyed would claim to have had some kind of "born again" experience, moral and ethical standards appear to be decidedly on the decline – even in our churches? Could it be that we are feeding, feeding and feeding, but failing to use what we have taken in? I have been to more than one church where many of the members seemed to be overweight – could it be they also were suffering from a form of spiritual obesity?

The Bible calls for us to be wise stewards, and we typically assume this refers to money and material possessions. I believe, however, stewardship concerns many areas of life, including our care and implementation of spiritual understanding that God entrusts to us. This means we need to learn how to apply our biblical knowledge in practical, everyday ways. Frankly, this is one of my motivations for wanting to share my insights about sheep with you

– not merely for you to be more informed about them and have a great appreciation for the Bible's sheep metaphor, but to encourage you to understand the joys – and inherent pitfalls – of being members of God's flock. Any shepherd will tell you that a bloated sheep is not an uncommon sight. As Jesus looks at His Church, I wonder if He also finds a form of bloating all too common as well.

Sheep can encounter other digestive dangers besides lush pastures. Like crawling infants and toddlers, sheep are not very particular about what they put into their mouths. This is another cause for the shepherd's constant vigilance.

I'm reminded of another TV commercial that ran for several years. In this one, two boys are debating who should be the first to try a new brand of cereal. Finally, they decide, "I know! We'll get Mikey to try it. He'll eat anything." And he did. For a shepherd, raising sheep is like overseeing a whole flock of Mikeys. If the sheep can't have rich, green food, they'll settle for weeds of all shapes and varieties – or virtually anything else they can reasonably chew and swallow.

Those times when the sheep are getting just the right mixture of feed can cause a shepherd to relax his guard. He must remind himself constantly to be wary of poisonous weeds that could jeopardize his entire flock. A wise shepherd will inspect a new pasture before allowing his sheep to graze. It always works best to weed out potential problems before they occur.

For instance, we had a pond on our farm. Visually, it was a wonderful scenic element on our property, but for our sheep it was a perpetual danger zone. The sheep loved to congregate around the pond as they grazed, but we knew there always seemed to be some new variety of vegetation appearing near the water's edge, so it was necessary to keep a close watch.

One summer a weed containing copper began growing there. Before we could identify the threat and remove the plants, several of the sheep ate some and became sick. Two of them died. Obviously, this further impressed upon us the need for vigilance to protect our ignorant, unsuspecting sheep.

Other than removing either the sheep or the noxious weeds, there was one other way of trying to keep the sheep on an acceptable diet. If they are provided with enough good pasture land, they generally will not bother with lesser quality plants. Sheep tend to eat weeds only if nothing better is available.

The point is not to make you an expert in how sheep eat, but rather to gain some valuable lessons from their haphazard feeding habits. Among the most obvious is the importance of monitoring our own dietary intake. Charlie "Tremendous" Jones, a popular motivational speaker and author, is a good friend of mine. He often states that five years from now any person will be the same as he is today except for the people he meets and the books he reads. My apologies to Charlie, but Ardie adds one additional category to that statement: the food we eat.

Every day we are confronted with an unbelievable variety of edible alternatives. We can eat moderately and sensibly, selecting foods that are nutritional and healthy, low in fats and sugar and high in fiber and vitamins. Or we can go to the other extreme and consume an unending assortment of junk foods, sweets, alcohol and tobacco – all of which ultimately will have a detrimental and toxic effect upon our bodies.

I haven't eaten any clover or alfalfa lately, but I must admit to having had a slightly bloated look around my middle. I remember attending a conference at a luxurious hotel. A waiter in the restaurant commented, "These Christians may not drink or smoke, but they sure can put away the food." I sometimes think that I, too, have become too proficient at this latter trait.

Nothing is more enjoyable than a satisfying meal. Physical intake, however, is just one aspect of our personal growth and development. I am reminded by a statement in John Piper's book, *Don't Waste Your Life*. He said, "God is most glorified in us when we are most satisfied in Him." In light of this truth, we need to be careful about what we feed our minds. Just as computers will respond only according to what has been programmed into them, our minds store the thousands of bits of information we feed into them; our thoughts and actions are influenced accordingly. The old computer adage, "Garbage in, garbage out," unfortunately has proved to be true too frequently for many of us.

Just as the Bible often refers to God's people as His sheep, it also provides guidelines regarding what our "food for thought" should be. In a verse we already noted, God promised, "Then I will give you a shepherd after My own heart, who will feed you on knowledge and understanding" (Jeremiah 3:15). Then, in Ezekiel 3:1,3, the Lord commanded the prophet to "...eat what you find; eat this scroll, and go, speak to the house of Israel," after which Ezekiel states, "Then I ate it, and it was sweet as honey in my mouth."

Jesus, our Good Shepherd who set the ultimate example for living, said, "My food is to do the will of Him who sent Me, and to accomplish His work" (John 4:34).

Contemporary society constantly assaults our minds and senses with a dazzling collage of messages, many of which have no godly origin. Despite this tempting and challenging environment, the Bible calls us to feed on a very specific mental diet. Joshua 1:8 tells us, "This book of the law shall not depart from your mouth, but you shall meditate on it day and night...." The man in Psalm 1 finds that "...his delight is in the law of the Lord, and in His law he meditates day and night." God tells us that to be of use to Him, we must cultivate appropriate thought patterns. We can only control that by what we feed our minds.

Long before a lamb is born, the quality of its life has largely been determined by what he has eaten – through its mother. Early in our experience with the sheep, we learned the importance of providing the proper food to our ewes if we expected their lambs to thrive. Sheep usually are content to eat hay, but six weeks before lambing time, our females would develop a strong yearning for oats. It was part of their natural process in preparing for the upcoming increase in food demand.

Even with the oats, however, the ewes sometimes struggled to produce enough milk for their famished lambs. Through experimentation and study, we soon discovered the moms and offspring would do the best when we fed the ewes a food supplement, a special protein feed that functioned as a milk producer. Once on this diet, the mothers never had any problems in meeting their lambs' milk quotas.

The difference was remarkable. Not only were the ewes better able to provide sufficient milk, but the lambs were much healthier and grew more rapidly. At those times when milk supplies were short, lambs would become weak and susceptible to illness; sometimes they would not survive. Both the thriving and ailing lambs served as notable examples of "you are what you eat."

Once again we find numerous parallels for us "people sheep." We know that an expectant or nursing mother should eat a balanced diet so her baby gets the proper assortment of nutrients. Spiritually speaking, we also have the responsibility of seeing to it that our human lambs receive the proper food for their minds and spirits. This means, I am convinced, a lot more than just delivering them to a church building once a week. We need to communicate the reality of Jesus Christ in our homes, through prayer and devotional or teaching times, and also by living out our convictions in front of them. This kind of influence and example will have an impact that endures far more than we could ever imagine.

Unfortunately, one of the greatest weaknesses that I have observed within Christian community is a general lack of preparedness to respond to the needs of "baby Christians," people who respond for the first time to the call of Jesus Christ as their Savior and Lord. We seem eagerly engaged in the business of producing converts, but not many of us are involved in the making of disciples, contrary to the mandate given to us by the Lord in Matthew 28:19-20.

I relate this to the parable of the sower that

compares one group of people to seed that falls on the rocks. It springs up quickly and blossoms, and for a time looks very good. But just as rapidly it wilts and dies because it did not become firmly rooted and properly cared for. Just as some of the lambs we raised would not thrive when they did not receive food of adequate quantity and quality, "babes in Christ" have an urgent need for proper spiritual feeding.

In my experience, this need often can be met most effectively through personal discipleship or mentoring, with a man meeting with another man, or a woman spending regular time with another woman, to establish a strong, trusting relationship, study the Bible, talk about how it applies to everyday life, and pray for one another.

For more than three decades I have had the privilege of meeting regularly with other men, sharing experiences and insights from our lives, and exploring the Bible, discovering how amazingly practical and relevant this sacred Book remains even though its writings were completed nearly 2,000 years ago. I continue some of these friendships to this day, even though in some cases we are separated geographically by thousands of miles. There is a unique joy and thrill in being a participant in the lifelong process of shepherding and nurturing needy, hungry lambs toward spiritual maturity.

In Minnesota, everyone looks forward to the coming of spring and the end of another long, cold winter. But for farmers and part-time sheepherders like me, the change of seasons was anticipated with special enthusiasm for another reason. Spring's arrival meant that the thick, hard, crusted layers of snow would vanish and once again the grass underneath could sprout skyward. No more need to lug feed for a while. Our four-legged lawnmowers would keep busy chomping on the eight acres of pastureland we had allocated for them.

The first spring rain always seemed special as well, since it signified the renewal of life in our part of the chilled upper Midwest. I was reminded of this some years ago, curiously enough, as I was driving in the South – from Chattanooga, where we were living at the time, to Nashville, Tennessee, about two hours away. The evening was warm and pleasant, and the windows of my car were down. It had just rained, bringing out the fragrance of flowers blooming along the highway. The valley we were traveling through was saturated with a delightful aroma. This aroused some dormant memories for me, momentarily transporting me mentally back to Minnesota and our gentle, trusting sheep.

It's interesting that the Bible compares our relationship with God to this kind of rain: "So let us know, let us press on to know the Lord. His going forth is as certain as the dawn; and He will come to us like the rain, like the spring rain watering the earth" (Hosea 6:30).

What an incredible image, isn't it – being refreshed and invigorated by the presence of God, just as the spring rain nourishes and restores the earth?

THOUGHTS TO CONSIDER AND DISCUSS:

1. When was the last time you heard a sermon on gluttony (if ever)? How do you think God would evaluate your personal eating habits? Consider what 1 Corinthians 6:19-20 and Proverbs 23:3 have to say on this subject.

2. How about the "diet" you have been offering to your mind? How are your present "feeding" habits affecting the nutritional needs of your intellect? Are you content with where you are in this regard, or do you see a need for some changes?

3. Next, consider how you have been feeding yourself spiritually? On one hand, are you pursuing ways to be fed sufficiently while, on the other hand, also taking steps to make sure you do not become bloated? How would you apply John 4:34 to your spiritual growth and commitment at this stage of your life?

Chapter Nine:
AN ADVENTURE
IN SHEAR DELIGHT

"...Like a lamb that is led to the slaughter, and like
a sheep that is silent before its shearers..."
— Isaiah 53:7

Sheep shearing. It's a good way of recovering part of the investment in your sheep, but it also provides a valuable service for the flock. As you can imagine, a thick coat of wool can be very heavy and hot. Not the recommended attire for a warm summer day, even for a sheep.

There is more to the shearing, however, than just grabbing a pair of scissors and rushing out to the sheep, cutting blades flashing in the sun. Sheep shearing requires specialized equipment and equally special skills. Therefore, even in areas where many sheep are raised, "baa-a-a-a barbers" are scarce and in high demand. It is truly a specialized craft. Unfortunately, this means you can't be as selective of the shearer as you might prefer to be.

One particular morning, it was my sheep that probably wished there had been a second choice. The only shearer available had just arrived and went

119

to work quickly. It soon became evident, however, that the fellow had been up much of the night and was enduring the lingering after-effects of his liquid intake.

I was amazed at the calmness of my sheep, even though the shearer's erratic movements sometimes resulted in more than just wool being cut by the razor-sharp shears. As the man worked his way through wool, seeming to hack through it, the sheep had every reason to panic and bolt. Yet they stood patiently. What a vivid example they were of the description in Isaiah 53:7, that tells about sheep being "silent before the shearers."

The only reason I did not push the fumbling craftsman back to his truck and off our farm was that shearers are so difficult to find – and even harder to schedule. There was no hope of getting another one any time soon, so I let him proceed and hoped for the best.

I winced as the man slashed away, transforming the shears into nearly lethal weapons. Blood dripped from one ewe's ear that had nearly been cut off. Others displayed lacerations on other parts of their bodies. The most serious injury was a severed tendon in another ewe's leg. Without any indication of regret or an apology, the shearer nonchalantly asked me to get him a needle and thread. He then proceeded to sew the sheep's tendon back into place as calmly as Ardie would sew a hem into a dress. To his credit, the repair work succeeded. In a short time, the injury healed and the ewe did not experience any ill effects from the runaway shears.

Years ago, when someone was tricked out of money

or swindled, people often commented that the victim had been "fleeced." After watching my sheep submit to the shearer without resistance or response, that term took on new meaning for me. Believe me, you don't want to be fleeced.

Throughout the ordeal, my sheep exhibited none of the anxiety that I was feeling. They did not even make a sound, while I felt like crying. The King James Version of the Bible translates Isaiah 53:7 in an interesting way: "as a sheep before her shearers is dumb...."

Shearing day was not always such a gruesome event, however. Sometimes it was funny – except for the lamb who wanted desperately to keep momma in sight. Ewe and lamb, as you would imagine, become very attached to one another from the moment of birth, and if danger is imminent, the ewe instinctively readies to protect her young one. Desiring both her affection, protection and nourishment, the lamb never strays far from mom. Whenever I read the poem that says, "And everywhere that Mary went, the lamb was sure to go," I wonder if Mary might have been the name of someone's ewe![4]

This intense family relationship can create chaos at shearing time. The contrast between a sheep with a full coat of wool and the same animal freshly trimmed is almost beyond belief. It would be like taking the stereotypical hippie from the 1960s, hair extending below his shoulders and boasting a full beard, and

---

[4] "Mary Had A Little Lamb" by Sarah Josepha Hale, Boston, Mass., originally published in 1830. Included in *Illustrated Treasury of Children's Literature* © 1955, Grosset & Dunlap, New York, N.Y.

giving him a complete shave and crewcut. For the ewes, the removal of the heavy wool was a relief, but the lambs did not always seem so appreciative. The mommas, minus their thick coats, temporarily confused their youngsters and caused considerable consternation.

"Ba-a-a-a!", they all bleated, which in lamb language for, "Where's my mother?!" You could almost see the anxiety etched on their faces. Both ewes and lambs voiced their concern as they called out to one another. Fortunately, when God got around to creating sheep, He trained senses other than eyesight to assist in this important identification process. Within a short time the crisis had ceased as parents and children reunited. The sudden quiet reflected their contentment, replacing the frantic bleating of just minutes before.

Over the years I have gotten to know a number of men and women who were separated from God, much as the lambs were from their mothers. In their own way, these men also called out, seeking to find where they belonged. In some cases, they tried the "gods" of money and success, while others attempted to find security and affection in people. Careers, power, and prestige served as other alternatives they tried. Yet it was only when they cried out to God and yielded their lives to Him that their "bleating" ceased and became replaced by peace.

Not long ago I was having lunch with an old friend. We had not seen each other in several years and were enjoying the opportunity to become reacquainted and catch up on what had been happening in one another's lives. My friend, Fred, had been telling me about how his business had prospered, making him richer materially than he ever could have imagined. He was reflecting on the vast amount of time he had invested in his career, but at the same time was admitting some key mistakes he had committed along the way.

Fred paused to take a sip of coffee, lowered the cup, and then leaned toward me. "You know, Ken," he said, "I have had a lot of success, but does it really matter?"

Somewhere along the way, while pursuing many of the treasures the world has to offer, he recognized that he had become like the church in the city of Ephesus, described in Revelation 2:1-5. Fred had abandoned his first love, turning his back on God, along with His perfect guidelines for peace and fulfillment in life.

But as he talked with me, he was declaring that at last he had recognized his need to repent and turn back to the Lord. Like a lamb bleating when it realizes it has become separated from its mother, my friend was ready to call again to his heavenly Father. And like the faithful, loving ewe, God also was waiting, eager to welcome a prodigal named Fred back into His fold.

All of us, in our own way, encounter situations like this during our lives. The Bible tells us we are "not of the world" (John 17:14-16; 1 John 4:4). However, sometimes the visible, tangible things of the world tear our attention away from the invisible, yet equally real promises of eternity. Fortunately, we have the assurance that Jesus Christ never changes. In His own words, He promised, "I am with you always." He never takes on a new look or develops a new perspective on life. Rather, He remains, "the same yesterday and today, yes and forever" (Hebrews 13:8).

I do considerable traveling in large cities and find it fascinating to observe the faces of people in transit. With the popularity of suburban living, millions of men and women spend numerous hours every week commuting to work and back to their homes. Just think about this: Rise early, get ready for work, eat breakfast. Hop in the car, or head for a bus, train or subway, and travel to somewhere in the downtown area. Work for eight or nine hours (often more than that), return to your chosen mode of transportation, and go back home. Upon arriving home, you try to spend a little time with the family, eat dinner, go through the mail, read the newspaper or watch some TV, and then go to bed – so you can start the cycle all over again the next morning!

As my friend had commented, "Does it really matter?" There is not much difference between us and the sheep, unless we can embrace the meaningful and purposeful lives that the God of eternity defines in His Word, the Bible.

There is an account in the sixth chapter of the book of Judges in the Old Testament. In it, Gideon used the fleece of a sheep to determine whether God wanted him to go to battle for the nation of Israel. In the story – seeking divine direction – he asked God to make the fleece wet with dew and the ground around it dry the following morning. Then Gideon asked for the opposite to occur: that the fleece would be dry and the surrounding ground wet the next day.

If you're like me, you may have wondered why Gideon selected a fleece, rather than a bear skin, the hide of a bull, or just an ordinary piece of cloth. He may have had other reasons, but it's likely he chose the fleece because of the uniqueness of the sheep's coat. It contains lanolin, a natural water repellant. If you have ever petted a sheep, you may have noticed a slightly oily feel to the coat; this was because of the lanolin content of the wool. We all have heard the saying, "Like water off a duck's back." You could say virtually the same thing about sheep.

It may be, then, that Gideon's request that God put the dew only on the fleece required a specific, supernatural act. Making the wool wet, while the ground around it remained miraculously dry. Then, perhaps wanting to make sure that the fleece was not defective, Gideon reversed his request, sort of like saying, "Just wanting to make sure, Lord. You know, I don't want to misread Your signals."

From this incident has developed an occasional practice that people – including some true followers of Jesus, as well as religious individuals – have come to refer to as, "laying a fleece before the Lord." Although I have tried it a few times myself, I have mixed feelings about the idea of putting out fleeces, asking for a sign from God as we try to make major decisions.

I'm convinced the Lord has given us sufficient insight into His will in the Scriptures, through godly counsel we can seek from fellow believers, and the inner peace (or lack thereof) we experience in the decision-making process. We certainly can overdo it. Not long ago, however, I felt impressed that such a "fleece" might be helpful in evaluating whether to relocate a man who reported to me.

Craig was ready to assume new responsibilities in a city hundreds of miles away, but only as soon as his house sold. His immediate supervisor, Jim, and

I agreed, knowing the financial burden a family can face if they move and have to find housing in a new area before their existing home is sold. Several of our other men had been caught in that type of dilemma, resulting in the unnecessary pressure of both mortgage and rental payments. We definitely wanted to spare Craig that type of problem.

Another concern was that his teenaged son was a junior in high school. Remembering our lesson with Janelle, I knew it could be even more difficult if the young man had to change schools one year before graduation.

I planned to suggest to Craig's supervisor, Jim, that we set a certain deadline for seeing the house sold. It would be a fleece of sorts to try and discern God's leading in this situation. If a buyer could not be identified by that time, Craig would not relocate until his son graduated from high school. An alternative plan would then be developed for the interim.

Later that day, his supervisor called me. Before I could mention my idea, Jim said, "You know, Ken, I've been thinking about our earlier discussions concerning Craig's situation. What do you think about setting August 15 (the exact date I had been considering) as the deadline for selling his house? If it doesn't sell by then, we'll have him stay where he is through the next year. What do you think?"

Almost word for word, that suggestion was what I had been prepared to recommend. I took it as God's way of confirming my own "fleece." As it turned out, Craig's house did not sell by the date we had set, so we postponed his new assignment, much to his and his son's relief.

Let me repeat: I am not suggesting that we seek to discover God's will in every matter by creating a series of fleeces. That would mock God and reflect distrust in His ability to guide us through His Word and the Holy Spirit. But as King Solomon is believed to have written, "there is a time for every event under heaven" (Ecclesiastes 3:1). He also wrote, "Commit your works to the Lord, and your plans will be established" (Proverbs 16:3).

I think about how God vividly demonstrated this to me and my family in 1996, not long after I had founded the ministry we call the Christian Network Team. About the same time, Ardie had also decided it was time to do something we had talked about for years – converting our home into a bed and breakfast. She certainly had demonstrated the gift of hospitality over and over during our life together, and getting into the hospitality business by turning part of our home into Country Cove Bed & Breakfast seemed like a logical next step.

Business start-ups cost money, however, even if the business is located in your home. As a consequence, cash flow is an ongoing problem. About this time another financial issue was about to present itself – Ardie reminded me that our auto lease was about to end and we would have to do something. I suppose that I must have responded with an "I know, I know," but the truth was, I didn't know. With the expenditures we had to make to get our bed and breakfast going, the last thing we needed was to take on a new car payment. I didn't place a fleece before the Lord to determine what we should do, but it was a concern that churned in the back of my mind.

I joined Ardie a few days later to go shopping for a new bed for the B&B at a local store, Slumberland Furniture. It was their anniversary sale, so while Ardie was diligently checking out their bargains, I registered for their anniversary drawing. After completing the registration form, I deposited it into the box and promptly forgot about it. We bought a comfortable new bed and arranged for its delivery.

It was about a week later and I was preparing for a trip to Tennessee to meet with some CNT members in Chattanooga. I received a message that the furniture store was trying to get in touch with me. I thought, "That's interesting. I must have won a bed or dresser or something."

When I called the store, they connected me with the marketing manager. "You had better be sitting down," he told me. "You have won a new Cadillac." Believe me, I was glad I was sitting down. Even now as I write this, I get numb. My lease was up so, even without a fleece, God solved my transportation dilemma for me – and in a way I could never have imagined or hoped.

Without a doubt, God knows our needs and He does provide, sometimes even before we can present our requests to Him. I have delighted to share this story with many people, both individually and when I'm invited to speak somewhere. This doesn't mean that the Lord always furnished Cadillacs, but He really does love and care for His sheep in ways that defy our understanding.

THOUGHTS TO CONSIDER AND DISCUSS:

1. The contrasting relationships of shepherds and hirelings to the sheep are instructive even for those of us who have never spent "quality time" with sheep. The deeply committed shepherd vs. the cut-and-run hireling in times of danger and hardship. Some observers have stated that one of our society's most pressing problems today is a generally low level of personal commitment. Why do we find it so easy to give up when circumstances get difficult in any area of our lives?

2. Revelation 2:4 tells us about how the church at Ephesus had "lost its first love." Being honest with yourself, what would you say is truly the first love in your life? What really matters most to you – and why?

3. What do you think of the idea of "laying a fleece before the Lord"? Have you ever tried that? In general, what is the process you use in trying to determine God's will for your life – and to arrive at important decisions? What does Psalm 32:8 have to say about this?

Chapter Ten:
SOMETIMES IT'S HARD
TO SEE THE BIG PICTURE

"But Jesus said, 'Let the children alone, and do not hinder them from coming to Me; for the kingdom of heaven belongs to such as these." – Matthew 19:14

Early in this book we talked about the fascination that sheep have with the "greener" grass on the other side of the fence. At times, we used barriers to restrict the access our sheep had to other areas, but occasionally the sheep confined themselves by their own narrow perspectives.

To make the task of keeping track of our sheep easier, we divided our pastures into sections, using fences and gates to guide the sheep into whichever areas we wanted them to use for grazing at any particular time. Sometimes we left more than one gate open to offer the sheep more freedom, allowing them to select from several sections of pasture. It was a simple matter to open a gate that, theoretically, would enable them to move freely from one area to another. Getting them to realize that their freedom had been expanded, however, was not always so easy.

Every once in a while a sheep would try desperately

to climb through one fence to get to another pasture, oblivious to an open gate less than twenty feet away that could have saved a lot of trouble. Rather than seek an opening large enough to pass through comfortably, the sheep would concentrate on an eight-inch hole in the woven wire fence, attempting in vain to squeeze through it.

The sheep would butt its head against the wire, trying to widen the small opening. Seeing its efforts frustrated would only cause the sheep to attack the fence more feverishly. Determined not be defeated by a barrier, the sheep could injure itself in its panic. There usually were two outcomes of this hopeless battle – the sheep would either accidentally discover the open gate, causing it to abandon the unyielding fence, or it would give up out of exhaustion and self-inflicted pain.

This pointless, agonizing exercise came about because the sheep had too limited a perspective of the problem. They apparently had an inability to see or grasp "the big picture," as the cliché goes. At times like these, I basically found that I was a helpless shepherd, unable to offer assistance since the sheep could not understand my suggestions or urgings for them to take an alternate route.

An analogy would be flying a small airplane over mountainous country. Below, you can see a car trying to pass a large truck on a curving, hilly two-lane road. As you watch, it becomes obvious that the driver of the automobile is hesitant to pull around the truck to pass, fearful of what might be approaching from the opposite direction.

Aloft in the plane, you can readily see when it would

132

be safe for the car to rush past the truck. You realize that if you could communicate from the plane to the driver, you could quickly resolve his or her dilemma, but that isn't possible. So you fly on, hoping the driver will remain patient and willing to wait until arriving at a point in the road where the view is clear enough to make the pass safely.

The pastor of my church gave a similar account in one of his Sunday messages. He and his wife had been enjoying a leisurely meal in a restaurant when a bird suddenly fluttered into the room. Apparently not hungry, the bird immediately began searching for an exit. Desperate to return to its accustomed outdoor habitat, the bird frantically bumped into walls, unable to find an open door or window. After several minutes of fruitless effort, the bird tumbled to the floor, bewildered and exhausted.

Fortunately for the bird, my pastor had a broader perspective on the situation. He walked over to the bird, picked it up and carried it out the door. Then he opened his hands, allowing the bird to go free.

All hindsight, we often hear, is 20/20. Today I can chuckle over the many times when I, much like my sheep, butted my head against artificial barriers of one sort or another, totally unaware of the open gate that stood just a short distance away. Handicapped by the inflexibility of my tunnel vision, I struggled to achieve the impossible, blind to the reality that God already had provided a better solution.

I have also learned that in some ways, getting older does not always make us wiser. In fact, we may become more rigid in our thinking. Sometimes a solution we had not considered must be presented in a dramatically different way for us to notice it. In one specific example, I observed a "lamb" leading the way for a "sheep."

It was at a men's weekend retreat in Green Lake, Wisconsin, where 300 men and a number of their sons had assembled. This event featured an abundance of good spiritual fellowship, but the emphasis was on evangelism. The weekend was filled with discussions of the Bible, singing hymns, and men talking openly and unashamedly about their lives – before and after Jesus Christ. It was evident that God was touching the hearts of many of the men in attendance, including non-believers who had come as guests.

On Sunday morning, as the retreat was drawing to a close, time was set aside for men to explain what the weekend had meant for them. Several expressed how inspiring the time had been. Most moving, however, were the brief testimonies of new believers who had just surrendered their lives to Jesus Christ during the past 48 hours.

One young man walked to the microphone and explained that he and his family had been praying many years for the salvation of his father. "He's a good man," he affirmed, "a real good man, but he wasn't a Christian. This morning, he invited Jesus into his life!"

We all shared in this excitement, especially when the young man's father strode to the front of the room, embraced his son, and recounted some of the events that had taken place during the weekend and the days leading up to it.

As wonderful as these testimonies were, they merely served to set the stage for one of the most emotional moments I have ever experienced. A young boy, not more than 12 years old, approached the microphone and began to speak. From his physical movements and appearance, it was obvious to all that he was profoundly disabled.

"Ever since I started going to school...," he said, before breaking into tears and sobs. Within seconds, his father was at his side, putting his arm around his son to help him regain his composure. After he had calmed down, the youngster haltingly explained that because of his disability, other children at his school teased him and made fun of him. "But I know...Jesus loves me...," he declared, "and I just...wanted you to know that He loves you, too!"

His simple declaration completed, the boy returned to his seat. While he had been standing at the front of the auditorium, an incredible hush had descended over the hundreds of men gathered there. As he sat down, however, the room exploded into applause as everyone saluted the young man's courage and the source of his strength, Jesus Christ.

Within moments, a burly man in his 40's walked quickly to the microphone. "Just now, because of that young fellow – I don't even know where he is sitting – and what he said, I am giving my heart to Jesus Christ," he announced, a broad smile bursting across his face. While going back to his own seat, the man located the boy, walked over to him and gave him a huge hug.

Unfortunately, words fail to begin to capture the thrill of that moment. As I looked around me, there was hardly a dry eye in the room. Some of the men openly wept, so moved by the events of the last few minutes.

Perhaps until that time, the burly adult had been resisting the call of Christ due to worldly concerns, pride or other reasons. He had probably believed that his way was a better way. Yet, through the simple, unvarnished words of a young boy, he finally came to a realization of how restricted his own perspective of life had been. The hope of Jesus Christ had been communicated in an uncomplicated, uncluttered manner, and at last the man found the gate to a better pasture. Perhaps the prophet was referring to this type of situation when he wrote, "...and a little child will lead them" (Isaiah 11:6).

Those who care for sheep see another example of the need for gaining a broader, fuller understanding of many situations. Have you ever seen sheep – or pictures of sheep – with long tails? You probably haven't, but sheep are in fact born with long tails similar to those of many dogs, except their tails are covered with wool.

From an appearance standpoint, sheep look better with short tails. However, the perspective of cleanliness is an even better reason for short tails. If left on, the long tails would collect waste materials, which, in turn, would attract flies. So the tails are shortened not long after the lambs are born. The process is not extremely painful, but it does cause some discomfort and even brief disorientation.

During our first years with the sheep, we had to cut the tails off with a knife and cauterize the wound. In the latter years, we switched to rubberized O-rings that cut off blood circulation to the tails, eventually causing them to fall off without harming the sheep.

For several hours after the O-ring was applied, a sheep would lose its equilibrium and experience difficulty when walking. But after a while, the lamb's balance would return, enabling it to move about with no problems. About ten days later, the tail would drop off, much like the placenta falls off a newborn baby.

If we had taken a shortsighted viewpoint, it would have seemed unfortunate to cause the pain, even though it did not persist for long. For the sheep's long-term well-being, however, it was definitely the most humane thing to do. It was far better than the assorted maladies that were certain to result from a long, dirty tail.

In 1972, I encountered a similar lesson in a drastically different geographic setting. My family and I had the opportunity to travel to Colombia, South America, where I went as a volunteer to assist with the installation of a telephone system for a jungle base camp established by the Wycliffe Bible Translators missionary organization. This base camp amounted to a two- to three-square-mile village situated at the edge of a dense, tropical jungle. From there, Wycliffe support personnel were sent out to work with primitive tribes, not only in Colombia but also in other adjoining South American countries.

Soon after we arrived at the base camp, I noticed that the Colombian nationals made extensive use of machetes – large, heavy cutting tools with broad blades that looked like oversized butcher knives. In their own way, these machetes were like the kitchen devices that cut, slice, dice, chop, and do who knows what else. The Colombians would wield their machetes with great skill, using them to chop wood, cut grass, butcher pigs, and even to kill snakes.

During the first few days of our stay at the camp, I frequently wondered, "Why don't these guys use axes instead of those heavy knives?" Having used an ax for some of the same tasks at home, I figured the Colombians were simply unenlightened. However, it took several months to get the phone system set up and operable, so I had many occasions to observe the machetes in action. It was amazing to see how skilled the men were with those knives, almost as if the tools were simple extensions of their arms.

Without a word of persuasion, I was gradually swayed to their way of thinking. Seeing the adaptability and multiple uses of the machete, I then started asking myself, "I wonder why we don't use machetes back home instead of axes?"

It occurred to me how quick I had been to judge the actions and customs of others, basing my conclusions solely on my own limited frame of reference. I too had failed to see the "big picture," the perspective of the people who had to work efficiently in a very difficult environment, not just for a few months but also for their entire lives.

This is another of the values that members of our CNT groups find – they can interact and share ideas about similar problems they face. As they do this, they discover new insights – perhaps about a different approach to a workplace issue, or the challenge of communicating the truth of Jesus Christ in their own unique business settings.

Being around older men who continue to cultivate a desire to learn and grow has always been a great source of encouragement. How refreshing it is to see the vitality and commitment of these men, some of them well beyond the years when many of their peers are opting for retirement. From men like these, I have learned that "retirement" really is not a concept advocated by the Scriptures, unless you happen to be a Levitical priest. In the business and professional world, where so many people are holding their breath as they anticipate retiring, the concept of non-retirement is a new perspective in itself!

My trip to South America was enjoyable, but over the years it has become abundantly clear to me that we can find everyday applications for the "big picture" principle wherever we are – at work, in the home, at church, or in the community. For instance, as a manager there were the unpleasant instances when I had to dismiss an employee. Sometimes the decision came after agonizing deliberation and prayer, knowing that someone's livelihood and security were at stake. However, in most cases I found that the dismissal would not only be best for the company, but also for the worker.

Perhaps he or she had proved ill-suited for the responsibilities; it would be unfair to everyone involved to have them remain in a position where they did not fit. At other times, the employee may have been irresponsible and undependable, despite several warnings. When it came time to terminate the worker, I always hoped the loss of a job would impress upon him or her the importance of responsibility and keeping vocational commitments with the employer. As the Bible clearly affirms, "If anyone will not work, neither let him eat" (2 Thessalonians 3:10).

In another work situation, it was one of my

employees that failed to see the big picture. Interestingly, this situation also had a link to missionary work. It occurred after I had moved from the telephone business to the small company where we serviced welding equipment and gas regulators.

It was a common practice for us to hire college students or children of missionaries for summer or part-time work. The jobs usually consisted of fairly simple manual assembly projects, with the part-timers working side by side with the regular employees. Usually this did not create any problems, but in one case a serious conflict developed between a young man and one of our permanent laborers.

The young fellow was the son of missionaries who were sacrificing the comforts of modern civilization to minister to native tribespeople in an African jungle. Labor standards are different today, but at the time we permitted smoking in this area of our plant since no flammable or explosive materials were used there. It happened that the missionaries' son was assigned a workbench next to a worker who was a fairly heavy smoker.

Offended and annoyed by the smoking, the young man mounted a large fan on his workbench. He positioned the fan to blow directly toward the opposite work area so that the smoke would go in the smoker's direction. Regrettably, the cigarette-consuming worker failed to see any advantage to laboring in a continuous breeze.

Eventually, I had to mediate in this dispute. Although I do not advocate cigarette smoking and realize it can be very bothersome for non-smokers, I felt then that the problem was unnecessary. It seemed ironic that the young man, whose parents had so readily relinquished the comforts of home to serve among strange people in a distant land, found it too great an imposition to temporarily endure the inconvenience of cigarette smoke. Understandably, he never earned a hearing from the co-worker to explain his Christian beliefs.

In my home, I have learned that discipline, as unpleasant as it often is to enforce, is another part of this "big picture." As much as a hug or a thoughtful gift, I have come to appreciate the value of discipline as an important way of demonstrating my love to my children. No question, I recognized the need to display my affection for them in overt ways, but I also had to show that I cared enough to correct them. We often have heard the statement, "This will hurt me more than it hurts you." Many times it did hurt me at least as much as it hurt my children to be disciplined.

Proverbs 19:18 urges parents to, "Discipline your son while there is hope." Similarly, Proverbs 22:6 exhorts, "Train up a child in the way he should go, even when he is old he will not depart from it." Both of these admonitions involve correction of some sort. Whether it involved a spanking, sending one of our kids to his or her room, or not allowing them to participate in a favorite activity may have caused temporary distress, but it was far better than having a wayward child who would grow up with no understanding of what was right and wrong.

THOUGHTS TO CONSIDER AND DISCUSS:

1. Think of a time when you worked long and determinedly, trying to solve a problem, only to discover later that you were so close to the solution that you virtually tripped over it. What prevented you from finding the right solution sooner?

2. Sometimes our greatest lessons come through painful experiences. Think of a difficult experience in your life that ultimately worked for your benefit. Describe the situation. Looking back, do you think the truth of Romans 8:28-29 applied there?

3. Why is it often so difficult for us to apply needed discipline in our families or on the job? How can discipline bring about positive change regarding work habits, personal behavior, or deeply felt attitudes? Look up Hebrews 12:5-11 and consider how it may apply to a circumstance you or someone close to you is presently facing.

Chapter Eleven:
YOU LEAD SHEEP, YOU DON'T DRIVE THEM

*"For you were continually straying like sheep,
but now you have returned to the Shepherd and
Guardian of your souls." – 1 Peter 2:25*

Eagles. Majestic, soaring sovereigns of the sky. It is a wondrous sight to see these living gliders riding the wind currents gracefully and with such ease, wings spread and virtually motionless. I had always admired these special creatures until one year when we received a fearsome, personal reminder that eagles are also birds of prey, ready to pounce on any small, defenseless animals.

That summer our sheep came under siege. A number of them, the lambs in particular, became victims of an unseen menace. I would return from work to find several of the animals with serious wounds on the tops of their heads. The flesh atop their heads gaped open, sometimes exposing a portion of their skulls. Their ears, usually at right angles to their heads or pointed diagonally upward, drooped as the skins pulled away from the jagged incisions.

This situation puzzled us. We knew of no animals

in the area that could inflict such injuries upon our sheep, especially ones that would concentrate their attack upon our flock's heads. Other parts of their bodies had not been harmed, so it seemed very unlikely that the assailant was a dog.

One afternoon a woman who lived nearby stopped at our house. She told Ardie she had been driving by when she noticed a lamb lying in the road, obviously injured. Ardie rushed to investigate and found the little animal lying still, in shock. The top of its head was gone. After carrying the lamb back to the barn, my wife put her nursing skills to work. She cleaned the wound and sewed it up as well as she could.

Ardie told me about the incident after I came home that evening. I was surprised that the lamb had been found in the road since I knew the fence in that area of the pasture was in good repair. There was no way the animal could have worked its way through.

Our veterinarian came out and agreed that the injuries could not have been caused by a dog. Studying the wounds and considering where the lamb had been found, we realized there was only one conclusion. The villains had to be eagles that had flown up from the St. Croix Valley, five miles to the east. It would have required an animal of their strength to carry the lamb, which weighed between 15 and 20 pounds, over the four-foot fence.

Over a one-year period we lost six lambs to the airborne attackers. It was a frustrating problem on two counts. We never actually sighted an eagle swooping down on the sheep, so there was no way to scare it off. At the same time, we could not keep the sheep confined to the barn indefinitely. When one of the lambs became injured, we would try our best to care for it, but each of the animals eventually died of its wounds.

We had one other reason for concern. Our youngest daughter, Jolene, was only a year old at the time and about the size of some of the lambs. We were afraid to leave her alone outdoors even for a brief time, not knowing when an eagle might choose to swoop down upon her. Being aware of an eagle preying on our lambs was a fearful enough thought.

The problem eventually resolved itself. When cold weather returned, the eagles stopped coming back and the remainder of our flock was spared.

In his excellent book *A Shepherd Looks at Psalm 23,* Phillip Keller points out that a sheep will not lie down to rest until certain conditions have been met. These prerequisites, he points out, include freedom from all fear, freedom from friction with other members of the flock, freedom from pests and parasites, and freedom from hunger. As you might imagine, those months became a very unsettling time for our sheep. Generally a fence offers enough security for a sheep, but the constant threat of terror from the air kept them anxious and restless that entire summer.

Even though the lambs seemed the primary target for the eagles due to their diminutive size, the ewes remained tense, sensing their inability to defend against the sudden invasions. The sheep's helplessness never was more evident to them – and us – than during those harrowing months.

It's interesting that the Bible, in presenting the promise that God will provide His strength for us in times of need, uses eagles as an illustration: "Yet those who wait for the Lord will gain new strength; they will mount up with wings like eagles..." (Isaiah 40:31).

We all have experienced times of anxiety, moments when we feared someone or something was poised to pounce and bring harm to us or someone we care for deeply. As I trust in God and His ever-watchful protection, I find great comfort in knowing that an enemy cannot come upon me unseen by my Shepherd.

Not long before we were to bid farewell to life in Minnesota and relocate to the rolling hills and warmer temperatures of southeastern Tennessee, I became friends with a police officer named Greg. His wife had committed her life to Jesus Christ and joined our church. Greg, although not a Christian and actually somewhat skeptical of his wife's faith, occasionally came to the Sunday service with her.

After I had known him for a while, I invited Greg to a businessmen's luncheon where a Christian executive would be speaking about his relationship with Jesus and what that had meant in his life. At the close of the talk, the speaker invited those attending to join him in praying a simple prayer to receive Christ if they had not already done so.

When I learned that Greg had prayed to invite Christ into his life, I was eager to get together with him to discuss it and see if he had any questions. If he had been a businessman, I would have stopped by his office or invited him to lunch. However, since Greg's "office" was his patrol car, my plan to follow up on him was a bit more difficult to carry out.

I had talked with him over the phone, but wanted to wait until I saw him in person to discuss such a personal and possibly sensitive subject. Finally, it occurred to me that maybe I could ride along with him in the police car for part of the day. That would give us plenty of time for a meaningful spiritual discussion. Greg said he was looking forward to talking with me, too, but first he had to get clearance from his supervisor before I could ride with him in the car.

One morning about 10:30 he called, excited to tell me that he finally had received the approval from his captain. "That's great, Greg," I replied, "but I'm going out of town in about two hours. I'll be gone for ten days, and I have a meeting to go to before I leave." Although he said he understood, I could tell by the tone of Greg's voice that he was disappointed.

My meeting was in the St. Paul suburb of Maplewood, at the international headquarters of the 3M Corporation. I went to the meeting, which ended promptly at noon. I hurried to my car, confident that I had enough time to go home, pick up Ardie, and drive to the airport. (This, of course, was in the days when airport security was minimal.)

As I pulled onto the roadway from the 3M parking lot, my car hesitated and then stopped abruptly. Discussing this incident afterward, Ardie commented she could not remember me running out of gas before, and I have never done so since. But this one time, without question, my car was out of fuel.

The car's momentum took it through the intersection, but then I came to a halt, blocking one traffic lane. "Oh, great," I thought, wondering where I could get some gas, knowing I might miss my flight. The fact that my car impeded traffic flow on a busy highway was an obvious concern as well. Then I noticed two patrol cars parked in a lot not far away. My first thought was that I might get a citation for obstructing traffic, but I walked toward the cars, hoping the officers might assist me.

As I neared the cars, I could hardly believe it, but one of the policemen was my friend, Greg. Immediately he came to my aid. He asked the other patrolman to pull his cruiser behind my car with the emergency lights on while he rushed me to the nearest gas station several miles away. To avoid any delay, he commanded the station attendant to give me a can of gasoline, and quickly we were headed back to my car.

During our brief ride together, Greg poured out his heart to me about some difficult issues he was facing in his life. I could tell how important it was for him to talk with someone he knew was interested and understanding. I thought about how, just 90 minutes before, I had told Greg that I would not be able to meet with him for at least 10 days. Apparently the empty gas tank was God's way of showing that He had a different plan.

After I returned from my trip, Greg and I began meeting once a week and had enough time together for him to discover many of the wonderful promises God gives us in the Bible. Before my family and I packed up to move to Chattanooga, Greg had received assurance of Jesus Christ as his personal Savior and Lord. Even though primarily by long distance, we kept in contact and maintained our friendship centered on Christ.

At last the time came for us to part with the sheep and our shepherding career. We had enjoyed having them and learning countless lessons from them, but we were ready to move to a new home and onto new things. As we sold the last of the sheep, we realized they had not netted us a monetary fortune, but the experiences they had given us were priceless.

I prepared to load the sheep into my truck and drive them to the stockyards in South St. Paul. I had made the trip numerous times, backing the truck up to one of the ramps at the huge livestock center. As I dropped the tailgate of my truck, the sheep, one after another, would venture out and walk down a narrow wooden walkway to an empty pen. I would be given a receipt for the sheep and drive away, knowing a check for the sheep would arrive within a few days.

Once in a while, after my part was done, one of the sheep would manage to sneak out of the building before the door closed and romp across the paved lot surrounding the stockyard buildings. Knowing how elusive those animals can be, I would just smile and think to myself, "I'm sure glad I'm not responsible for catching that sheep!"

The day we officially dispensed with the remainder of our sheep remains vividly impressed upon my mind. As it happened, Bob Tamasy was in town that evening on business and stayed in our home. I invited him to ride along for the grand finale, although we had no idea at the time that one day we would collaborate on a book about our life with the wooly friends.

For one last time that evening, I back up to the large building that temporarily would become their new home. As I opened the rear gate of the truck, the sheep hesitated briefly – as they often did. However, once one of them stepped out and headed down the ramp, the others dutifully followed. There were no good-byes. To be honest, I shed no tears and had no regrets.

It had been a good, instructive and often entertaining fourteen years with the sheep, but as King Solomon wrote, "To everything there is a season, and a time for every purpose under heaven" (Ecclesiastes 3:1). The season for sheep had come to a close.

Fortunately, life for me and my family has been deeply enriched by our association with our animals. And thanks to them, the Bible's many references to sheep, lambs and shepherds have new, deeper – and often, more personal – meaning for me.

As my wife, Ardie, points out, one of the primary requirements for a healthy flock of sheep is a good source of regular food. The shepherd moves the sheep from one pasture to another to accomplish this goal. This not only keeps the sheep well-nourished, but also protects the land from overgrazing and becoming depleted.

Christ, our Shepherd, is doing this for us as well. New circumstances, whether it involves location, vocation or both, stimulate growth and development. The Bible says, "The steps of a righteous man are ordered by the Lord" (Psalm 37:23). As the perfect, all-knowing Shepherd, the Lord rotates our pastures as needed to keep us healthy and stimulated.

So when I get restless in my circumstances, I am reminded to follow the Shepherd, even when this seems to mean remaining in a holding pen. As I wait and trust, I find that His supply is adequate and my faith grows in the process.

What about you? Do the Bible's sheep passages now make more sense to you? Can you see – and understand – yourself as a sheep? How would you rate your relationship with the Shepherd? When He calls, are you listening for His voice?

I'm reminded of a favorite story that famed news commentator Paul Harvey has often recounted during the Christmas season. It concerns a man whose family was getting ready to attend church on Christmas Eve.

"No, I'm not going with you," he told his wife and children. "You're welcome to go if you like, but I don't see any point in it." With that he sat back in his favorite chair, picked up the newspaper and settled in for a quiet, relaxing evening while his family was away.

Outside it was cold and snowing, so the man found the inside warmth especially pleasurable. A few minutes later, however, he heard the sound of tapping outside the house. At first he ignored the noise, assuming it was probably a branch being blown against the wall by the wind. But when the sounds persisted, he decided to take a look.

Going to his front door, he peered out and noticed a flock of birds flying toward the illuminated window of his house, trying in vain to get inside. Taking pity on the scared and shivering creatures, the man tried to think of a way to help.

Behind the house was a small barn. "I know," he told himself, "I'll open the door to the barn, get the birds' attention, and lead them into the barn." To his dismay, however, he could not get the birds to notice him. They were intent upon the light that they knew meant warmth on the other side of the window. Although the man was offering them safety and shelter, the birds were bent on solving their problem their own way.

"How can I get them to notice me and realize that

I can help them?" the man mused aloud. "Oh, if only I could briefly become like them, be a bird for just a little while. Then I could tell them about the shelter they would find in the barn."

At precisely that moment, the bells of the nearby church began to toll, announcing the start of the Christmas Eve service. The timing, the man realized, was no coincidence. For the first time he understood that just as he would have liked to become a bird so he could deliver the feathery flock from their plight, Jesus Christ, the Son of God and the Good Shepherd, had come to help a flock of another kind. He had humbled Himself in becoming a man, so that men, women and children all around the world could know about the single, eternal answer to their problems.

In the beginning was the Word, and the Word was with God, and the Word was God.... And the Word became flesh, and dwelt among us (John 1:1-14).

A few years ago I was in Chicago for a business management seminar. I had rented a car and was following the directions to the meeting hall. For some reason, one small but important detail in the directions had been omitted, and I spent nearly thirty minutes searching for the building.

I eventually stopped and asked for directions. To my surprise, I had driven past the location several times, but had not been aware of it. I had been in the neighborhood all along without knowing it! I felt foolish, having overlooked the obvious.

It is my hope that this book has been both enjoyable and enlightening. Hopefully, the next time you read a Bible passage about sheep you will smile and nod knowingly, a bit wiser from our brief time together with the sheep.

There are many reasons for a shepherd to count sheep. Perhaps one has become stuck in a fence, or has become cast. It might have broken a leg, or just has overeaten and is suffering the consequences. As I close, however, I would like to ask you a question: Can you identify personally with being one of sheep being counted by God?

Do you know the Shepherd, Jesus Christ, personally? If Jesus were to call His flock home today, are you certain that He would be including you? The Bible states, "And all the nations will be gathered before Him, and He will separate them from one another, as the shepherd separates the sheep from the goats" (Matthew 25:32). Similar to how I was as I searched for the building in Chicago, have you been in the neighborhood of salvation, but have overlooked the obvious: your *personal* need of the Savior?

If you have any doubts about your relationship with the Lord, I would suggest that you repeat a simple prayer like this one: "Dear God, I realize that I am a sheep in need of the one true Shepherd. I have gone astray, breaking your laws, and I sincerely ask for Your forgiveness. I am inviting Jesus Christ to come into my life, to lead me as my personal Shepherd. I ask you to take control of my life and guide me. Amen."

Now, if you have said that prayer, let me urge you not to stop there. Get in touch with another follower of Christ and tell him or her of your decision. Seek out a church or a Christian support group that believes and upholds the Bible as the inspired Word of God. And ask God to bring another person into your life to serve as an "undershepherd," to challenge you and help you grow and mature in your faith. I can assure you that God will be faithful in fulfilling your request.

If you already are a follower of Jesus, perhaps you see yourself as one of the sheep who has strayed from the flock. You have heard the Shepherd calling, but you know you have been ignoring Him, choosing to go your own way. Perhaps you have fallen for the lure of the greener grass, or you have been stubbornly trying to kick while you are on your knees. And now you are sensing an inner longing to return to His fold.

Jesus' love for you today is as strong as it has ever been. He is waiting for you to return. "For you were continually straying like sheep, but now you have returned to the Shepherd and Guardian of your souls" (1 Peter 2:25).

Perhaps the best way to restore your relationship with your Savior is to repeat the prayer of another man who knew a lot about sheep from personal experience. In Psalm 51, King David repented of his own sin and waywardness by praying,

Be gracious to me, O God...according to the greatness of Thy compassion blot out my transgressions. Wash me thoroughly from my iniquity, and cleanse me from my sin.... Against Thee, Thee only, I have sinned, and done what is evil in Thy sight.... Create in me a clean heart, O God, and renew a steadfast spirit within me.... Restore to me the joy of Thy salvation, and sustain me with a willing spirit.

THOUGHTS TO CONSIDER AND DISCUSS:

1. It can be extremely frustrating to have all the pieces of our lives seemingly in order, only to have the unexpected turn them into turmoil. What are your fears or anxieties concerning your career, your marriage, your family, or your future in general?

2. Sometimes God will not take "No" for an answer. When was the last time you saw Him turn an apparent disaster into an opportunity, as He promises in Jeremiah 29:11?

3. Throughout this book, we have considered numerous illustrations about sheep to show the many ways they are similar to people. Which of these examples has been most meaningful to you? Why?

4. In what ways do you depend upon the Shepherd? How would you compare your role as a "sheep" to Christ's role as your Shepherd? Consider the promise God gives in Jeremiah 33:3 – how does this relate to your life and relationship with Him as a member of His flock?

WISDOM FROM THE FLOCK

- *The grass is NOT always greener on the other side of the fence.*

- *Know who it is that you are following – and why.*

- *You lead sheep, you don't drive them.*

- *Sheep reproduce sheep, not the shepherd.*

- *Even when situations seem hopeless, don't be too quick to give up.*

- *Don't try to teach a sheep to roll over – it's a waste of time. (Corollary: If you find yourself belly-up, yell for help!)*

- *You can't remove the wool from your own eyes; someone must do it for you.*

- *Having parasites removed isn't fun – but it's necessary.*

- *You are what you eat, so consider your menu carefully.*

- *If life gives you indigestion, get out of the weeds.*

- *It's hard to see where you are going when your head is stuck in a bucket.*

- *It's easier to find an open gate than to have to fix a fence.*

- *If you're oblivious to the obvious, you'll be obstructed by the obscure.*

- *Discipline often hurts, but lack of discipline usually hurts worse.*

- *To find out if you're a true shepherd, turn around – is anyone following?*

Would you like to learn more about
Christian Network Teams (CNT),
a growing network of
business owners and executives
who meet monthly for mutual counsel,
spiritual support and accountability?

Visit our web site,
www.christiannetworkteams.org,
or send an e-mail to
cntmn@juno.com

Pass The Blessing On...

"Pursuing Life
with a Shepherd's Heart"

If you know of a book store, church or reseller
who would like to make this book available;
please have them contact:

publisher@rivercitypress.net

RIVER CITY PRESS
Publishing "Life Changing Books"
4301 Emerson Avenue North
Minneapolis, MN 55412
1-888-234-3559